ABERDEEN
AN
ILLUSTRATED
ARCHITECTURAL GUIDE

W A Brogden

AN illustrated architectural guide to the Granite City is long overdue and those interested in this fine City can glean from these pages the historic record of its architectural growth. It allows the reader to put in perspective the ever changing built environment, to consider the achievements of the past and to draw from this rich source of inspiration when considering the quality of future development.

Our illustrious forebears have set high standards for the present and future generations to follow. Let us face the challenge with their same enthusiasm and expertise so that our city will retain its renowned character.

The support of the City of Aberdeen District Council for this publication is greatly appreciated.

JAMES C LYON
President
The Aberdeen Society of Architects

Published by

The Royal Incorporation of
Architects in Scotland

and

Scottish Academic Press
33 Montgomery Street
Edinburgh

ISBN 7073 0488 1
An RIAS/Landmark Guide
Series Editor: Charles McKean
Design Production: Dorothy Steedman and Bill Brogden

Front cover: A cappriccio of 1840 by Thomas Mackenzie showing Aberdeen's ancient buildings and recent additions by Smith and Simpson. The frame is based on Bishop Dunbar's tomb.

Brown

Aberdeen is the paragon of Scotland. Its banks bathed with the glittering streams of Dee, and her walls shaded with fertile cornfields . . . the buildings of this city are framed with stone and timber; facing the sun, and fronting this pleasant harbour; the streets also are large and spacious, and the walls strengthened with towers and buttresses of stone.

Although written over three hundred years ago, this description is still apt. It is remarkable that even though Aberdeen vastly increased its size in the 19th century, virtually building a new city, it yet retained its basic and recognisable character. It is no less remarkable that it has managed to hang on to that character today.

A city is its buildings, and, since buildings unlike citizens do not at all mind being stared at, photographed and pointed to, they are the most accessible key to Aberdeen's character. Through them one can come to know much of the nature of the Aberdonian himself.

Aberdeen is in the north-east of Scotland, some five hundred miles north of London, and one hundred and twenty from Edinburgh. Being thus remote, it had to look after itself somewhat. Besides being the focus for the rich lands of Deeside, Donside, the Mearns and Buchan, Aberdeen is also a seaport and, until the beginning of the 19th century, the harbour was the real entry to the town. Therefore Gotenburg or Amsterdam were as handy for the trading Aberdonian as British ports, and a deal more lucrative. Chief exports were for many years stockings, especially to Germany. This was succeeded in the late 18th century by cloth, especially linen, manufacture, and this still continues. Granite export began in the 18th century too, at first paving for the streets of London, then

Brogden

Top: Central area from harbour.
Above: Assembly Rooms Portico.
Opposite: Aberdeen from the south with the Dee and North Sea.

The city's motto *Bon Accord* came about when, in the Wars of Independence, the Aberdonians supported Robert Bruce. The castle and town was garrisoned with supporters of Edward I and Balliol. The townspeople attacked the garrison during the night and killed them all, the watchword for the night being Bon Accord. In 1319 King Robert Bruce granted Aberdeen a beneficial Charter which included the Forest of Stocket. The considerable profits under the Charter came to the Burgh of Aberdeen and are the basis of the Common Good Fund.

INTRODUCTION

Union Street and the Castlegate from Union Bridge.

finer stone for building worldwide. The tea trade by Aberdeen Clipper — the world's fastest — occupied much of the 19th century, until the very lucrative trawl fishing industry established itself in the 1880s, to be superceded itself by oil exploration a hundred years later. Now for the next wave of prosperity. . . .

Roads and canals were vastly improved around 1800 but it was the coming of the railway that established the easy connection with the rest of Britain. The competition of the major companies to see which was the fastest between London and Aberdeen established the fast and reliable service which allowed the Monarch to spend considerable time on Deeside and for government to carry on by regular visits from Ministers. It also meant that Aberdonians could open their offices in London and elsewhere, and attend to business from time to time by the Sleeper.

If distance moulded Aberdeen's character that character was expressed in granite, the sharp, bright hard stone that keeps even quite elderly buildings looking new. On dull wet days even white granite cannot stop the city appearing dull and wet also. However, in sunshine Aberdeen literally sparkles.

For most of its history Aberdeen was confined to an irregular series of streets around St Katherine's Hill. It extended from the market place in the east, the Castlegate, to St Nicholas Church and yard on the west, and from the Harbour northwards by Broad Street and Gallowgate to the Gallow Hill and then to Old Aberdeen.

In the early 19th century it broke out of this pattern, and spectacularly. The period between 1800 and 1900 witnessed phenomenal growth in population, in prosperity and this was accompanied by a love of good buildings.

According to the English poet and man of letters Robert Southey writing of Aberdeen in 1819, *the Scotch regard architectural beauty in their private houses as well as in their public edifices much more than we do; partly because their materials are so much better.*

Until about 1850 Aberdeen's taste in building was decidedly plain, even austere. This suited granite very well indeed and local builders perfected the art of very fine masonry whose joints are almost invisible lending the earlier buildings a handsome, monumental aspect.

First with Trinity Hall and then Christ's College a more romantic quality comes into the City's building suggesting a fondness for history, for allusion, and for more ornament. As the 19th century turns into the 20th the architecture becomes more varied, bolder, and as workmen gained confidence and skill so remarkable buildings such as Marischal College were added to the city's sights. Houses became fancier too as a glance at Golden Square and the nearby

Granite

It is the fashion to belaud Aberdeen for its white and clean appearance. Its white and grey granite when well dressed, have a fine sparkle in the sunshine, and when there is wind enough to clear away the smoke, and the light is full upon the spires, and they look as if they were built of white marble. My old friend and fellow Ruskinian, James Walker the Dean's brother, described the Town long ago in a set of verses as:
The silver City of the Sea.
a fine and apt simile, but there is another side to the picture. In some lights, and under other conditions, the granite looks cold, hard, repellent and colourless. John Morgan, Memoirs.

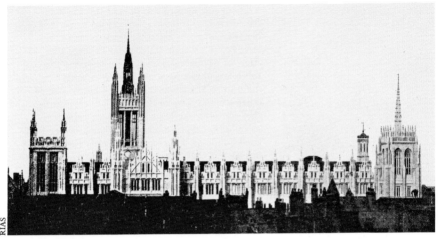

tenements on Rosemount Viaduct amply testify.

In the 1920s, and especially the 1930s, there was a return to a taste for simple monumental buildings. Rosemount Square or the Bon Accord Baths, or the Donside Housing Schemes show this in granite. After that material was abandoned in the 1950s because of cost, concrete structures became more common: being fewer, though large, these buildings have not significantly altered Aberdeen's character; and in many cases they are of intrinsic merit anyway, such as Hazlehead housing scheme. The buildings that have come with oil and its related activity are for the most part on the edges of the city where architects have been able to build in a modern idiom without worrying that their work spoils the character of existing neighbourhoods.

How to build in an established and handsome city is a great problem which we are specially aware of now. A feature of Aberdeen architecture — both before Southey noticed it, and afterwards — is that it is truly civic — the design of buildings and the layout of the town itself were characterised by long and drawn out discussion. In many cases years passed between design and final execution, in which time the merits (or otherwise) of various schemes were thoroughly debated. That brings a certain conservatism, a disinclination to change quickly, and therefore Aberdeen keeps its character. These discussions continue today.

Architectural guides are often thought to be difficult — perhaps because in the past they have used such curious terms and little illustration. By concentrating on great buildings and great periods they are apt to leave the user to puzzle about the layout of streets, the design of houses — the bulk of towns, the neutral or ordinary buildings.

Marischal College with old Broad Street, 1939.

The Name: Aberdeen
The origins of the name Aberdeen often puzzles visitors, as well as natives. Apparently it derives from the *mouth of* (the aber) and the river Deen; but as the rivers are Don or Dee and certainly not Deen, there is confusion. Very probably the name comes from the Denburn, the stream that runs through the city and on which very early settlement took place. Thence Aberden, and in the early days it was often spelled that way.

But what about Aberdon as Old Aberdeen was known when St Machar's was a functioning cathedral. Because of the Cathedral and then the College, Aberdon entered Europe, and modern Aberdonian derives from Hector Boece's latinising of the name in the 16th century. But for a long time Aberdon has also been known as Old Aberdeen.

Well, that introduces a further complexity. The district of Old Aberdeen is often, and affectionately called the Alton, or Altoun, or Aultoun, which sounds to modern ears like a Scots version of Old Town. However Alt' tuin is Gaelic for *stream by the dwelling*, or *colony* and refers specifically to the settlement where Powis Burn crossed College Bounds.

This guide attempts to present the whole of Aberdeen and to make accessible all its periods of history, and all its building types. So the Guide is arranged in sections which show first the Central Area, or Mediaeval Town; the pattern for this still survives and can be appreciated in a walk. Similarly the history, the character, and the patterns of the other sections have determined their arrangement and they can form the basis for walks or drives.

Not all buildings could be included, not even all good buildings. However, it has been the object to include the characteristic buildings of each district or period. Sometimes building types are seen to best advantage in a particular location. For instance tenements in Rosemount or bungalows on Anderson Drive. It is hardly meant to suggest that all others be ignored. But it is hoped that having got the basics a reader can make connections and fill in gaps for himself. Then this guide can be just a reference book. If any glaring omissions are noted, and any mistakes, do bring them to our attention so that they can be rectified in future.

Organisation of this Guide

Not all buildings mentioned are illustrated. The small numbers adjacent to the text are keys to the maps. Where possible the entries follow the order of name, address, date, architect (if known) and then description. The index should make cross reference easier.

Right of access

Almost all the buildings in this Guide are visible from a street or road, and many are open to the public. However, many are private and therefore not open to the public, and readers are requested to respect the occupier's privacy.

Albert Dock.

David Brown

Brogden Collection: RIAS

Castlegate

The great market place is very beautiful and spacious, and the Streets adjoining are very handsome and well built, the Houses lofty and high; built not so as to be inconvenient, as in Edinburgh; or low, to be contemptible, as in most other places. But the generality of the citizens' Houses are built of Stone four storey high, handsome Sash-windows, and are very well furnished within, the citizens here being as gay and genteel, and perhaps, as rich, as in any city in Scotland. Thus Daniel Defoe in the early 18th century.

The heart of Aberdeen, and its architectural focus is Castle Street, familiarly known as the Castlegate: the marketplace since the 12th century. It is a long rectangular space set high above the Dee between Castlehill and St Katherine's Hill.

RCAHMS

Top: Castlegate as painted by Hugh Irvine of Drum, 1803.
Above: Mercat Cross and north side of Castlegate, late 19th century state.

1 **Mercat Cross**
John Montgomery, 1686
By far the finest thing of its kind in Scotland, wrote Lord Cockburn in 1841. The ceremonial and symbolic centre of Scottish mediaeval burghs, Aberdeen's Cross is the most modern — and the most splendid. Above the arcade, a parapet divided into twelve panels contains armorial bearings of the Crown and the City, and particularly fine bas-relief portraits, in oval frames, of the Stuart Monarchs from James I to James VII, (a trifle too crisp for their supposed age: the Cross was restored by John Smith in 1820). A column

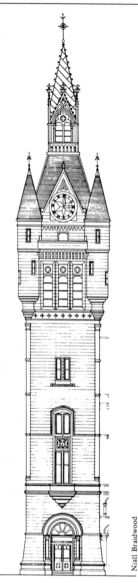

Town House, West Tower.

Niall Braidwood

On Monday *August 23rd we were invited into the Town Hall where I had the freedom of the city given to me by the Lord Provost. Parchment containing the record of admission is, with seal appending, fastened to a ribband and worn for one day by the new citizen in his hat.* Dr Samuel Johnson, 1771.

with Corinthian cap, wreathed by thistles and roses in bas-relief supports a coloured and gilt marble unicorn. Originally some hundred yards further west, the Cross was moved to this quieter end of the square in 1842, when the arcades formerly *Hucksters' booths* and latterly the Post Office, were opened.

2 Town House

From 17th century, Thomas Watson

Nothing survives of the original tolbooth which existed near Weighhouse Square, between Shiprow and the Harbour Offices. Following a 14th century royal grant allowing a new Tolbooth to be built anywhere in Aberdeen (with the exception of the centre of the market place) the canny Aberdonians chose the *corner* of the Castlegate: in 1615 they constructed the great square tower with corbelled bartizans. Now largely obscured by later additions on the Castlegate, its full height of three storeys can be appreciated from Lodge Walk. In 1627 a belfry and spire was added, although the present spire dates from c. 1726 when the first clock was installed, the present clock dating from 1817. Its main function was a prison. Tours of the Tolbooth cells and Town House are available.

The Town House proper lay to the west of the tower. Repaired in 1670, rebuilt in 1729 when a staircase was added to the west, permission was granted to build a wing to the *east* in the later 18th century thus making the roughly symmetrical composition which is recorded in Irvine's painting of 1803. The expansion was not to accommodate extra municipal business: rather it was for the New Inn with, on the top floor, two great rooms for the Masonic Lodge, the eastern lit by a splendid Venetian window.

New Town House

Peddie and Kinnear, 1868-74

This confident, even authoritative Victorian Town Hall won a competition and unbalanced the scale both of the old Castlegate and the new neo-classical city of Aberdeen. Its self-conscious mediaeval Flemish style was chosen to reinforce the memory of Aberdeen's ancient trading links with the Low Countries, and its construction ushered in a new phase in Aberdeen's architectural development which culminated in the new front of Marischal College.

The Tolbooth tower at the east end is *balanced* by a great tower at the west end of the building. The ground floor arcade gave access to offices, with the entrance to the Sheriff Courts at the centre. A dwarf arcade represents the first floor above this, while the main function of the building, the Town's Halls, are

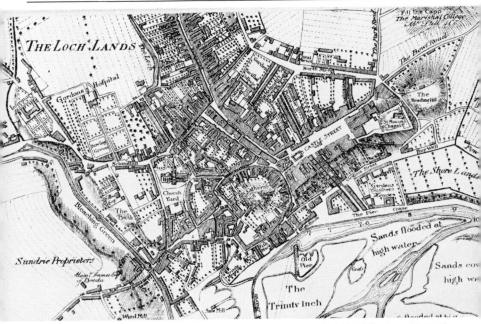

accommodated in lofty splendour at the top, and
rising into the high roof.

3 **Bank of Scotland**
James Burn, 1801
The former Banking Company in Aberdeen, this early
essay in white granite set a pattern for urban buildings
which was followed through much of the 19th
century. Pre-eminently a bank, the two upper floors
above united by giant Tuscan pilasters sit on a
rusticated base. The deep overhang of the cornice is
very much in keeping with the *primitive* and elemental
nature of the Tuscan order. Much of William Smith's
later interior work survives.

The Castlegate has always been ringed with houses,
some of them the town houses of rural grandees. The
house demolished to make way for the Bank of
Scotland was **Pitfodel's Lodging** c. 1530, probably
the first stone house in the city, three floors tall, with
turrets partly for ornament and partly for defence.
The Earl Marischal's Hall next door was even
grander. A quadrangular building enclosing a
courtyard, it presented a tower to the Castlegate, with
a large garden extending soutwards to roughly the line
of Virginia Street. It must have been very grand. The
Marquis of Huntly took up residence there at the
outset of the Civil War, with *twenty-four* gentlemen in
attendance.

Eastwards was **Rolland's Lodging**, 16th century
with twin gables facing into the Castlegate dated

Brogden

Top: Aberdeen in 1773 from
George Taylor's Survey.
Above: Bank of Scotland from
Lodge Walk.

9

Above: Castlegate Well.
Right: Salvation Army Citadel.

When the cistern was first erected a brass gilt statue three feet and a half high was ordered for the top, and four *antick* figures with three faces each were to be placed at the corners of the cope, the cost to be added to the water debt, already amounting to £1571; but there was some delay in setting about casting the statue and figures, and the zeal of the citizens having cooled they resolved to be content with the wooden model of the *Mannie* which had been prepared. With a coat of gold leaf it looked very well for a time. . . .

Mary, Queen of Scots stayed as a guest in the Earl Marischal's Hall and from the windows (with a charm typical of the 16th century) she was obliged to witness, in the square opposite, the execution of Sir John Gordon of Findlater, thought by many to be her lover. Gordon was executed by the *Maiden*, Aberdeen's patent guillotine, after his capture at the battle of Corrichie, 1562. This brought to an end the Gordon rebellion, with the Cock o' the North, Chief of the Gordons himself dying of a heart attack on the field. The *Maiden* itself can be seen on the upper floor of Provost Skene's House.

c. 1630. Said to have been the first purpose-built tenement, it was demolished in 1938.

4 Castlegate Well
Plainstanes, 1706

A rectangular stone fountain on a raised plinth, this was a central part of Aberdeen's water supply. On special holidays, the masks at the corners worked as fountains. It was removed to the Green in 1852, when the lead statue of a figure known as the *Mannie* was made to replace the original. In 1972, the Well was moved to the restored *Plainstanes* (originally dating from 1760) opposite the Townhouse. Merchants used the Plainstanes as an outdoor Exchange, strolling together to discuss business or politics. Those thus addicted were known as *Peripatetics*.

5 Salvation Army Citadel
James Souttar, 1893-96

The 1789 Record Office (a handsome, five-bay Georgian building with a wide centrepiece under a pediment, preferred to Robert Adam's even handsomer and rather taller design) was replaced by the most dominant building in the square — the Salvation Army Citadel, (realising an earlier Gothic design by John Gibb for this site). By the late 19th century the Castlegate (especially the Barracks and suburbs to the east) had become ripe, indeed a trifle

10

over-ripe: a part of the town which stern and upright folk did not care to frequent. The Citadel was built in the heart of temptation, and the symbol of strength and redemption Souttar chose was the castle, namely Balmoral. No wonder Ceres, gazing complacently across the Castlegate, from atop the Clydesdale Bank, is mistaken for Victoria. The Citadel challenges the Town House, and from any point along Union Street, forms a theatrical climax for the city's eastern end.

The North Side of the Castlegate contains a row of granite fronted houses of two to four storeys (the tall chimney stacks and back gables are of Seaton brick), the ground floors commercial. This pattern has obtained here from at least the 18th century, although most of the present buildings appear to be early 19th century. **17 Castle Street**, c. 1760s, possibly the work of William Law, is built of Loanhead granite, the coarse grained (and consequently weaker), beige coloured stone used before the fine, very hard white granite became available. The large arch with a shield in the crisp architraves leads to **Albion Court,** one of 19 courts which opened out of the Market Place. Originally these led to the gardens of the houses along the Castlegate, subsequently built upon. Albion Court, for instance, led to four further houses. Recent archaeological investigations in this particular *backland* has shown traces of this development occurring as early as the 17th century. **Albion** and **Smith's Courts,** along with **Peacock's Close** are undergoing a revival largely through the efforts of the Peacock Printmakers, who have established a lively workshop and museum in the old St Andrew's Cathedral school. Across Smith's Court are the Art Space galleries, and next to them is the new **Seabury Building,** for St Andrew's Cathedral, by Ron Gauld, 1984. The block between Peacock's Close and Chapel Court was renovated by Oliver Humphries in 1984.

Brogden

Smith's Court.

Futtie's Port

There were two gateways to the city in the Castlegate. Futtie's Port in the south-east corner led under the Castlehill to Futtie.

The hinge-pins for the footgate survive in the gable end of the late 18th century house in 4 Castle Terrace. Futtie's Port and **Castle Hill** leads to what little remains of the **Castle.** There was a fortress here as early as the 13th century, but (according to Gordon of Rothiemay) the citizens took it down in King David II's time and *least at any tyme thereafter it should prove a yock upon the townsmen's necks, they rased it to the ground, and, in place thereoff, builded a chappell which they dedicated . . . to St Niniane, hopin by that meins that the hill being converted to a holy use,*

Mr Francis Peacock was for the space of sixty years, the much respected teacher of dancing in Aberdeen. He had always a strong *predilection* for drawing, but never took a pencil in his hand to attempt anything in colour, till he was about 40 years of age. He received his instructions in London, and particularly from Francis Cotes, who was esteemed a good artist, and died about the year 1770. Mr Peacock copied with great delicacy and truth, and thereby greatly promoted his improvement in taking likenesses in miniature, which he painted at moderate prices. To a genius for music and painting, he united the unaffected manners of a gentleman. No man possessed a more nice sense of honour.

He assisted in the first formation of the weekly subscription concerts, and with great ability joined the band in the Orchestra, both on the violin and violin cello. Late in life he published a treatise on dancing, well written, and as well received by the public and the teachers of that part of genteel education.

Walter Thom, *History of Aberdeen,* 1811.

THE CENTRAL AREA

Futtie is also called Footdee, —
the Bowdlerizers insisting that
Futtie is a vernacular corruption of
Footdee. In the 18th century, it
was called Fittysmire: the
birthplace of the celebrated
architect James Gibbs. However
Futtie is likely to be the real name,
and it is the one generally
preferred.

James Souttar was apprenticed to
Mackenzie and Matthews at the
age of twelve and stayed on in
Aberdeen for eight years. Then in
1860 he got a job with Digby
Wyatt in London before setting off
on an extensive continental tour.
He lived in Sweden from 1863-65,
married there, and published an
*History of English Gothic
Architecture*, in Swedish.

He returned to Aberdeen and
practised here with his assistant A.
E. Melander until 1871 when
Melander returned to his native
Sweden. Souttar's Aberdeen work
includes the Imperial Hotel (from
1869), the tenement blocks 96-120
Rosemount Viaduct of 1887, and
his masterpiece — the Salvation
Army Citadel in the Castlegate,
1893-96.

*it would be unlawful to attempt to imploy it to a
profayne use. . . ."* That noble sentiment prevailed
until the Civil War, when General Monk's troops
occupied Aberdeen and enclosed the chapel within a
four pointed fort of earth and stone walls and
bastions. The material for this was removed from the
choir of St Machar's by the Cromwellians in 1654.
The south-east bastion still survives, but St Ninian's
Chapel was demolished in the late 18th century when
the Barracks were constructed.

7 **Virginia and Marischal Courts**
City Architects Department, 1969
Two slab blocks, of nine and eighteen storeys, whose
heavy concrete frames define the individual flats — all
with balconies. The rock-face granite and concrete
panels on the gables are meant to be a sculptural
response to building at this scale, as are the great
sculpted concrete supports on which the blocks stand.
Like residents of other high blocks in Aberdeen the
people who live in Virginia and Marischal Courts do
so quite happily and comfortably and, despite their
size, the blocks contribute positively in the
scenographic ending of Union Street. They do not sit
ill on Castlehill.

Virginia and Marischal Courts
from the East.

12

Justice Port
In the north-east corner was the other gateway from the Castlegate, the Justice Port (now Justice Street) which led either to the Gallowhill, or, by the north side of Castlehill, to the Heading Hill, where witches were burnt (the last as late as the 1740s) and decapitations took place. Then the heads, or other parts, of the most notorious criminals were exhibited on the gate of Justice Port. In the ordinary way, the Justice Port was an alternative entrance to the city from the Brig o' Balgownie and the north.

8 **St Peter's Roman Catholic Church**
Justice Street, James Massie, 1803
Extended by Harry Leith in 1814 and approached through the rather fine gateway of an 1843 tenement building, the ensemble is centred on, and entered from Chapel Court. St Peter's interior is quite plain, with wide, pointed windows of simple tracery. The altar piece is worth noting, as are the Stations of the Cross, and Sacristry enclosure, in best '50s style.

Below: Old Catholic School, latterly the Shiprow Tavern.
Bottom: Marischal Street.

9 **Old Catholic School**
62-86 Constitution Street, 1833
Probably John Smith
Sadly dilapidated for so fine a building. A single-storey composition of central block with flanking wings, it is an interesting variation on a standard Palladian layout with shallow pitched, overhanging roof. Entrances to either side in the form of classical porches.

The Rows
Besides the Ports, and the Courts and Closes, the Castlegate was connected to the rest of Aberdeen only by Rows, at the west end of the square. Not much wider than a close, these were Huxter Row, Narrow Wynd (both obliterated in later improvements) and Exchequer Row which still exists but in an enlarged form. Exchequer Row, and beyond it the Shiprow, became terribly overcrowded and insanitary, and this area was among the first to be declared unfit. The buildings began to be demolished from as early as the 1890s, very little now remaining.

10 **Marischal Street,** 1767
The transformation of Aberdeen into a modern city began with the creation of Marischal Street, on the site of the Earl Marischal's Hall. This led (regular, broad and straight) from roughly the middle of the Castlegate to the Harbour. The steepness of the natural slope of the ground was overcome by building up the street on arches and embankment.
Bannerman's Bridge, half-way along, by William

13

Law, 1767, carried the new street over what became Virginia Street — replaced when Virginia Street was widened. On either side of the road are rational and regular Georgian houses. In the north half they are identical: five bays wide, and three storeys tall, built of Loanhead granite, with classical cornice, raised margins to the sash windows, and a central doorway.

One of the least altered is **No. 30** Provost Young's House, 1770 by William Dauney, an uncle of Archibald Simpson. A central passage leads to the half-oval staircase at the rear. On each floor are two major rooms (to Marischal Street) and two minor rooms, wood panelled, with mantlepieces as shaped stone surrounds without a shelf. The details and craftsmanship are of a very high standard.

44 Marischal Street, William Smith, 1780
Below the Bridge are houses said to be by William Smith, father of John Smith, the first City Architect, whose design is more varied: **No. 44** has a very grand drawing room running from front to back.

The Age of Improvement
If a bridge across the Dee to Kincardineshire could have been constructed from the bottom of Marischal Street, or even if a roadway could have been constructed along the north edge of the river, then Aberdeen might have been satisfied. As both these expedients were not then feasible, the building of Marischal Street appears only to have whetted an appetite for improvement. In the late 18th century, the main entry into the city from the south led up the steep Windmill Brae, across the Bow Brig over the Denburn, through the Green, past the slum of Putachieside, and thence into the city by the Shiprow and Exchequer Row. The entry north was either through Old Aberdeen, down the Gallowgate into Broad Street — or across the Links to the Justice Port.

At a public meeting in 1794 it was decided to ask the Roads Surveyor, Charles Abercrombie, to prepare a report on the best ways of linking Aberdeen to the hinterland. He preferred three choices: a new bridge over the Dee, a new road along the Dee mentioned above, or two new roads: one from the south-west to run from *the entry of the Damhead Road towards the Chapel of Ease and be carried from thence eastward nearly in a straight line along the grounds on the north side of Windmill Brae, across Denburn, and the Back and Correction Wynds, and through St Katherine's Hill and the Narrow Wynd, until it joins the west end of the Castle Street*; and the other to run from the Town's Mealmarket to join the Castlegate just east of the New Inn.

Of Abercrombie's choices, the Council selected the

James Burn of Haddington, as he is usually surnamed, was an important architect to Aberdeen. he practiced in Haddington from 1777 as both a builder and an architect, which he continued until the 1820s.

His contributions to Aberdeen are the Aberdeen Banking Company of 1801 in the Castlegate, perhaps the original terrace design for King Street and the splendid castle-like Bridewell which sat athwart Rose Street from 1809 to 1869. The jail, never really required, and even more unnecessary after Smith rebuilt the Town's jail in Lodge Walk, was a landmark in the western part of the town. Its small windows, and castellated top is echoed, somewhat, by the Broadford Works.

two new roads. In 1799 the Trustees advertised for designs. Early in 1801 seven designs for forming the two streets, with the necessary several bridges for the sewers, indicating *the proper heights of the fronts, and construction of the roofs of the houses,* were put on display in the Town House. David Hamilton's scheme was the unanimous choice, and he immediately began work on bridging the Denburn.

One of the Trustees' principal tasks was to negotiate with the owners of buildings or land in the way of the new streets and, when they had bought out the existing owners to secure the best terms and buildings in accordance with their Scottish powers as landlords. The Trustees' main *architectural* problem was to establish the style and disposition of the new buildings, and to persuade their fellow citizens to bid for the feus and build upon them. It was ten years before building began on the south street or Union Street as it became. But by late 1803, most of the land for King Street between Castlegate and North Street was in hand.

Union Bridge in the early 1820s when the South side, now the site of Littlewoods and Boots, was unbuilt.

David Hamilton (1768-1843) is famous for his work in Glasgow, beginning with Hutcheson's Hospital, 1802-05. His winning competition entry for the new approaches to Aberdeen and for Union Bridge is his first known work. His errors in establishing the levels of Union Bridge, and his consequent departure from Aberdeen may be put down to lack of experience. His subsequent career in Glasgow was distinguished.

Family of John Smith

Creators of the Granite City

John Smith (1781-1852) was the son of a builder and architect, responsible for several houses south of Bannerman's Bridge in Marischal Street and the young Smith trained with him before going to London. In 1807 he succeeded Thomas Fletcher as the Trustee's Superintendent of Works, which office later became simply City Architect, and his first work was in King Street. Through his own abilities and his family's influential connections he soon established an extensive private practice.

King Street from 1803
King Street is really beautiful. Their granite wrought as they now work it, when fresh, is not much, if at all, inferior to marble. Lord Cockburn, 1841.

Designs for both sides of the new street had been requested from David Hamilton and James Burn. Hamilton was presumably too busy with the Denburn Bridge to oblige, and Burn supplied elevations and outline plan only, unfortunately lost. A drawing by the Trustees' Assistant Thomas Fletcher survives, showing a composed terrace, with centre blocks, advancing in two stages, and further blocks at the ends. Fletcher's job including redrawing the relevant part of Burn's design for the prospective feuars, thus making a sort of contract drawing.

8-10 King Street, 1805, and **12-14** King Street, 1810, were built for Robert Catto from the Burn-Fletcher scheme, and form a fragment of the intended terrace. 8-10 King Street stands a storey higher than its neighbours, and breaks forward as well, and constitutes slightly more than half of the south terminal block; both are based on 55 Castle Street, 1803, perhaps also by Burn.

The opening up of King Street presented few physical difficulties, but there was a protracted quibble with the Society of Advocates about boundaries, access and compensation. The first feu, taken up by Alexander Brebner (or Bremner) at the

11

corner of the Castlegate proved smaller when the site was cleared and measured than had originally been stated. The difficulty was resolved in 1809 but a valuable six years had been lost.

The plain difficulty was that no one would bid for the stances. The Trustees began to be worried, and by New Year, 1804, had Burn make designs for *different lengths of fronts and elevations*. Although they continued to profess their desire to *preserve regularity and uniformity in the street it had occurred to them that the plan of the buildings should afford as much variety as might suit the ideas of different purchasers*. Fletcher made drawings as the Trustees directed, but in future matters were resolved more by negotiation. Maximum and minimum heights were laid down, as well as the slopes of the roofs, and standards of stonework. But any ideas of an architecturally coherent terrace, as became standard in Edinburgh after 1800 was, as far as Aberdeen was concerned, impossible.

Thomas Fletcher retired in 1807, replaced as Trustees' Assistant by *Mr John Smith Junior, Wright and Architect*, soon to be known simply as City Architect, or latterly *Tudor Johnnie* from his fondness for, and skill with, 16th century styles. He began with Brebner's corner block, which he built c. 1810. At the corner he introduced a personal contribution: a curving bay of superimposed tripartite windows and a simple blocked cornice at top, which *turns the corner* and faces diagonally into the square. This trait became a feature of Aberdeen architecture.

Aberdeen University

Archibald Simpson (1790-1847) returned from London in 1813 where he had worked with the interesting and forward looking Robert Lugar, and latterly David Laing, before travelling to Italy. Simpson's people were clothiers in Broad Street although a maternal uncle was William Dauney architect of 30 Marischal Street. Although Simpson had designed Morrison of Auchintoul's house while still in London, his Aberdeen practice was slow to develop, but by 1816 he was well established.

Smith and Simpson were professional rivals but there was no animosity involved. In King Street they worked in creative collaboration, almost as musicians might in developing variations or responses to the lead of the other. Often they were consulted about the same project and each would give designs — sometimes other architects would join the *competition* — and the results were judged by their clients. In this fashion each had had sufficient business to carry on a successful practice.

Simpson who lived in Bon Accord Square was musical and enjoyed the friendship of artist James Giles: being unmarried, he was more a citizen at large. Smith's house was in 142 King Street (set behind the terrace of his houses) and he was busy with family and his official duties. Both were intimately involved with the Mechanics Institute, the precursor of Robert Gordon's Institute of Technology.

Brogden

St Andrew's has strong links with the Episcopal Church in America, through Bishop Samuel Seabury of Connecticut (1729-96). Seabury was born in Connecticut and educated at Yale College in New Haven. He was Episcopalian rector in Westchester, New York and during the Revolution he was obliged to join the other Loyalists in New York. After American Independence, Seabury was elected first Episcopal Bishop. He sailed for England to be consecrated but was kept waiting for over a year. In 1784, however, he received a Christian welcome in Aberdeen where he was consecrated by Bishop Skinner, whose own consecration had been nearly secret. Thus began the long connection between the Scottish and American churches. This connection was to have been commemorated in the grand new Seabury Cathedral, which was to be built in Broad Street. The Wall Street Crash put paid to that, and its designer, the Aberdonian Sir Ninian Comper turned his attention instead to redecorating the interior of St Andrews, called the Seabury Memorial restoration and funded by the American Episcopal Bishops. The baldacchino with skinny, gilt *barley sugar* columns is a most spiritual version of the Roman original.

Previous page left: King Street in the 1830s.
Right: St Andrew's Episcopal Cathedral.

Below: West side of King Street.

12 St Andrew's Episcopal Cathedral
King Street, Archibald Simpson, 1816
The Episcopalian community acquired the centre stance in the King Street *terrace* as the site of their new chapel. The result was a perpendicular style building: small, with little embellishment apart from the outsize crockets at the front corners with gothic detail in Craigleith sandstone. The style and the material underlined the distance between the Episcopalians and their Presbyterian neighbours. The chancel end was added in 1880 by G. E. Street, and Sir Robert Lorimer provided the porch in 1911. The splendid interior in delicate white Gothic, the arms of the States of America adding brilliant colour to the aisle ceilings is by Sir Ninian Comper, from 1936-43.

13 Medico-Chirurgical Building
Archibald Simpson, 1818
The two-storey and attic centre consists of a severe, four column Ionic portico in granite. The stances to either side had it written into their feu charters that the buildings would be set back in line. Accordingly, when John Smith built the County Record Offices, 1832-33 to the south, he made a three bay *wing* to Simpson's building, but he also enhanced the whole composition in his design. The County Record Office *main front* appears to be a terminal block to a building entered through Simpson's portico: yet it is given the proper individuality by Smith, his doorway between two advanced bays ornamented with pairs of pilasters.

15 Aberdeen Arts Centre (formerly North Church)
John Smith, 1829-30
On the north side of the Medico-Chirurgical building Smith added another *wing* but his *termination* block is the North Church which many consider to be his masterpiece. Designed to be seen from many angles, it is specially effective from the north with its striking tall and flat-headed portico of Ionic columns, with the tower growing out of it (terminating in a rather

Live

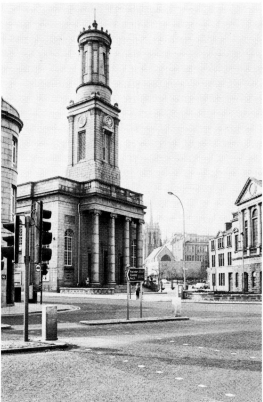

Livesley

The Medico-Chirurgical Society was founded in 1789 by twelve medical students led by the future Sir James McGrigor, founder of the Army Medical Corps, for the purposes of *mutual improvement*. The new building was designated to house their valuable library and a meeting place. An obelisk to McGrigor stands in Duthie Park.

Left: Aberdeen Arts Centre.
Below: Arts Centre and Old Tolbooth Spire from King Street.

Livesley

attenuated homage to the Tower of the Winds in Athens). Smith's characteristic attention to detail is exemplified in the way the bays are set off by pilasters, the segmented windows within further set back, enhanced by the thin strip of glazing which seems to carry this recession deeper yet. Some of Smith's interior survives in the vestibule and stairs, but visitors are struck much more by the smooth and crisp '50s style of the conversion to the City Arts Centre; theatre above, and the meeting rooms below.

Smith built most of the east side of King Street between 1825 and 1830. The houses, now standard, are by no means identical. The two south of St Andrews have sections of cornice ornamenting the first-floor windows, and the chimney stacks of nos. 30 and 32 are fully granite, with a coved cornice. The ground-floor arches have been subsequently obliterated, but it appears from a fragment surviving at the entrance to no. 32, that rusticated granite blocks were used. North of St Andrews, there are several surviving runs of ground-floor arches, **No. 48**, with the original glazing bars, unusual in being domestic. **Nos. 50-56**, 1840s, completes the terrace

The *Hinge of the City* in 1840 with Mercat Cross in its original position, the Old Town House, Smith's new front to the Tolbooth, Simpson's Bank, and Insurance Office, Gillespie Graham's block, two Smith houses, and the Record Office, Medico-Chirurgical Society and North Church group. On right is Bremner's Block.

1-4 King Street
Archibald Simpson, 1839
Originally built for the North of Scotland Fire and Life Assurance Company, it is three storey (its arcaded ground floor later replaced), the windows ornamented, and a panel set above the centre. Its neighbour, by James Gillespie Graham, 1836, has five fairly narrow bays with an off-centre entrance. The two-storey upper section, dominated by giant doric columns, sits on an arcaded base. It is a rather un-Aberdeen looking building (indeed it might have been lifted from Graham's, Moray Place, Edinburgh). Graham and Simpson quarrelled over the design.

14 **Clydesdale Bank** (formerly North of Scotland Bank)
5 Castle Street, 1839-42, Archibald Simpson
The hinge of the city, replacing the New Inn. There were various competing deigns for this site, but Simpson's very modern curved corner porch with giant Corinthian columns (with Giles' statue of Ceres comfortably sitting on top) could not have been beaten. This corner is balanced by two two-storey wings of very crisply detailed granite blocks, the windows being set in sunk panels, a modilion cornice with a balustrade above. Much of Simpson's original interior survives.

Beyond North Street, King Street continues with
three-storey buildings, then smaller, less regular,
granite houses, predating 1820 and designed by Smith.
Much original detail and ground-floor shop
arrangement survive. Yet King Street never really
fulfilled its expectations as did Union Street. Its
character beyond the Aberdeenshire Canal, (now a
railway line at Roslyn Terrace), remained suburban or
rural. At the junction with the old canal is A. H. L.
Mackinnon's Fire Station, 1897, tending to Edwardian
free-style. 352 King Street is William Smith's
Italianate Boy's and Girl's Hospital of 1869-71, now
part of Robert Gordon's Institute of Technology.

The dual carriageway ring road replacing North
Street caused much unnecessary damage but, in an act
of inspired conservation, the block opposite the North
Church was removed and rebuilt at the corner of the
widened street by Grampian Region Architects
Department.

18 St Katherine's Centre
Jenkins and Marr, 1937
Vying with Gray's School of Art as the best mid-20th
century building in the city, and obviously inspired by
the contemporary geometric architecture of Holland its
material (granite, of course) and its confined site
allows it to sit happily with its neighbours. The front
to North Street is severe and blocklike, only its rows
of square windows suggesting its date but the flanking
elevation to Shoe Lane shows its true character now
that the fine buildings in 18th century Queen Street
have been demolished. The glazed stair tower, the
front block, and the much larger back block are
moderne.

Above: St Katherine's Centre from
Shoe Lane.
Left: Fire Station as drawn by
Curtis Green.

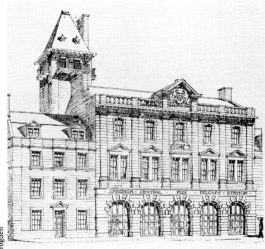

Arthur H. L. Mackinnon
(1870-1937) was trained by
Matthews and Mackenzie and
showed early promise, particularly
the Fire Station, King Street of
1897, and his ingenious tenement
and hall connection of Union
Terrace to Rosemount Viaduct. He
enjoyed a prosperous maturity and
was active in professional bodies.

Broad Street in its heyday, c. 1840.

RCAHMS

19 Broad Street

Judging from the Rothiemay map of 1661, the Broadgate leading north to Gallowgate was then the most prominent street in Aberdeen, site of the Greyfriars, several noble town houses, and Marischal College. With its extension, the Gallowgate, it led to the north city gate at Mounthooly. Broad Street is now entirely 20th century, embodying the collective wisdom of planning in this century: namely the desire to create Open Space; for similar activities to be grouped together in Civic or Cultural Centres, or Housing Schemes; and for these to be connected together by efficient modern roadways.

In Victorian times the Broad Street district was overcrowded and insanitary and in the 1880s the first steps were taken to alleviate the worst of this. A wrecked remnant of the ancient street remained between the Wars, when some grand notions were canvassed. The Seabury Cathedral was proposed here in the 1920s; and a new Town House was proposed in the 1930s to stand opposite Marischal College. The 1952 Chapman and Riley Plan for Aberdeen, **The Granite City**, proposed a Cultural Centre, with a new Art Gallery and Library on the west side of Broad Street, Provost Skene's House turned into a City Museum, and Marischal College (which naturally had to be tidied away with the rest of the University in Old Aberdeen) to become the home of Robert Gordon's Institute of Technology. Broad Street was to become a *Place*.

The Cultural Centre became a civic centre, the Broad Street *Place* was created, and Queen Street

The great romantic, poet, and Greek patriot **Lord Byron** was born plain George Gordon. His parents had met and married in Bath. Catherine Gordon of Gight near Aberdeen, was an heiress, and mad Jack Byron was an obviously attractive, if dangerously unsuitable, match. When young Byron was three, his father died, having run through his mother's money already. Mother and son returned to Aberdeen in 1791 and lived in lodgings in Broad Street. Although an income was found for them by family trustees, Byron's prospects were poor: lame himself, his home comforts were meagre, and his mother's affections and attention varied alarmingly. Still, they managed: he attended the Grammar School, then nearby in Schoolhill, and learned the Bible with his nurse. He visited the old Brig o' Balgownie, and imagined the worst. However he left Aberdeen when only ten years old in 1798 to take up his quite unexpected title and estates.

became part of a large open *precinct* with much civic
gardening. On the south side is the Police
Headquarters and adjacent on the raised platform is
the Sheriff Court (backing with the jail into the Town
House and High Court) by the City Architects
Department, 1972. At the corner of Broad Street, with
the north half raised on *pilotis* is the Town House
Extension, 1975, by City Architects Department
which contains the Council Chamber: all clad in silver
gray mosaic tile. Town Planning theory has been
much revised since then.

20 **St Nicholas House**
From 1962, City Architects Department
One of the earliest tall buildings in the city, still
among the most prominent, and clearly influenced by
Lever House, New York. Originally to have been clad
in curtain-walling (a light skin of glass and enamelled
steel panels) it was thought that masonry was more
suitable for the Granite City, hence the concrete and
mosaic tile, with granite for the ground floor.

21 **Provost Skene's House**
From 1545
A garden court with T. B. Huxley-Jones's
sculpture/fountain, provides the setting for Provost
Skene's House, also known as Cumberland House,
from the six-week residence there of the Duke of
Cumberland in 1746. It is all that survives of the
formerly densely packed neighbourhood, and had
fallen on evil times (being known in the 19th century
simply as the Victoria Lodging House). Its fate might
have been the same as its neighbours, but for a timely
expression by Queen Elizabeth in 1938 which saved it.

Top: Old Greyfriars *Windoe.*
Above: Lower Broad Street, 1972.
Below: St Nicholas House.
Left: Provost Skene's House.

George Keith, 5th Earl Marischal (1553-1623) was a zealous reformer, a student first at King's College and later in Geneva, and from his succession to his titles a servant of James VI and the reformed church. He was commissioner for executing laws against Catholics, and for apprehending the Catholic Lord Huntly. In 1593 he founded Marischal College in Broad Street in the former monastery of the Greyfriars, and thus established the curious rivalry, which obtained in Aberdeen for 250 years until the University of Aberdeen was established in 1860.

The earliest portion is the three-storey Lumsden wing whose steep gable faces the court. It is in this wing that the older rooms are to be found — notably the Painted Gallery of 1626, which contains one of the most important cycles of religious painting in Scotland. The principal wing was regularised by Sir George Skene of Rubislaw, a wealthy merchant trading with Danzig, soon after 1669. The plasterwork in the 1676 bedroom and the panelling in the Georgian Drawing Room are particularly splendid. *Open to the public: Guide book available.*

22 Marischal College
Founded 1593
Established in 1593 by the Earl Marischal, as a Protestant alternative to King's College, Marischal College was first established in the redundant Greyfriars Monastery; it joined Kings in the unified University of Aberdeen in 1860. The original buildings, added to in the 17th century, were grouped around a large courtyard behind Broad Street. Greyfriars Church 1518-32 formed the west side of the court: an example of late Scottish Gothic by Alexander Galloway, with wide pointed windows and buttresses.

Simpson's *new* College in 1840.

They boast much of their new Marischal College, Confined amidst paltry buildings, its position is bad, it has no architecture, and its erection implies the destruction of the old buildings, which sets all they will do utterly at defiance. Lord Cockburn, April 1839.

Aberdeen District Council

By the early 19th century the two Colleges had
deteriorated both as institutions and buildings; and in
1837 Archibald Simpson designed a new Tudor-style
quadrangle in white granite behind the original houses
of Broad Street. The centre was marked by a tower,
behind which were large teaching rooms, with smaller
rooms, served by an arcade of perpendicular arches,
grouped around the quadrangle. In the centre of the
court was a large pink granite obelisk (now removed
to Duthie park). Greyfriars Church was left occupying
the west side, and a gateway led into the crowded and
picturesque Broad Street, then occupied, among others
by regular, 18th century, three-storey houses, a cistern
house with pediment, clock and urn finial; and a tall
17th century house with prominent turret, a boyhood
home of Lord Byron.

Left: Mackenzie's first scheme
with Mitchell Tower and *restored*
Greyfriars Kirk.
Below: Marischal College,
Greyfriars, and the Town House.

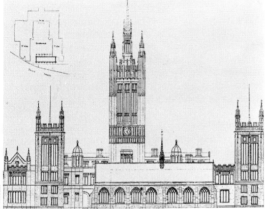

Duncan

Brown

Marischal College Rebuilding
1891, A. Marshall Mackenzie
Mackenzie had prepared a scheme for extension to the
College, with a new and more magnificent towered
gateway and a cleaned and restored Greyfriars
Church. The scheme approved, it was sent to the
Council Improvements Committee, accompanied by
two further options: to build an entirely new College
elsewhere, or to abandon the old Greyfriars Church
for a new one and create a wholly new Broad Street
facade to the College. This latter idea aided by the
Mitchell Bequest to fund a new examination hall
beyond Simpson's original (rendering it a magnificent
vestibule) as well as an extension to the central tower
(resulting in the Mitchell Tower, nearly 80 metres of
neo-Gothic granite which still dominates the City
skyline) was adopted. The ancient Greyfriars and
Broad Street had to go.

The Marischal College facade fronts the second
largest granite building in the world after the Escorial
in Madrid. It is an extraordinary technical

*The Marischal College is a very
ordinary building in bad order. They
have a shabby church, a hall and a
library that are merely decent, some
lodging rooms for students, the
schools, and two or three houses for
Professors. But they are all in very
bad order. The stairs are not so much
as plastered.* Alexander Carlyle,
1765.

*The buildings are very old and
very ugly, but a grant has been
obtained from the government and
subscriptions raised in the city to the
amount of £25,000 with which a new
college is immediately to be erected on
the site of the present.* The Scottish
Tourist, 1836.

Brown

Brogden

Top: Marischal College Gate.
Above: 6 Upperkirkgate.
Below: Destruction of Jameson's House.

Aberdeen City Library

achievement, for the stone is put through paces never thought possible. The skyline fretwork is almost insubstantial, granite interspersed with stiffly ruffled gilt flags. The shorter tower at the south-east angle is the entrance to the new **Greyfriars Church** — whose east window incorporates early 16th century tracery from its predecessor's *faire windoes.*

Upperkirkgate
The north end of Broad Street is intercepted by Upperkirkgate. The corner buildings were remodelled with corner turret, and gothic, be-crocketed arch (raised on the wallhead of the Students' Union), at the turn of the century.

Most of Upperkirkgate is late 18th or 19th century and presents a varied streetscape similar to the Castlegate. 42 Upperkirkgate is the only house which has the once typical characteristic of gable facing the street. The original entrance was from the east, either by way of a pend or perhaps a garden.

23 No. 6 Upperkirkgate
R. G. Wilson, 1899.
An interesting exercise in homage to Scottish architectural heritage, incorporating bits from older buildings (two 17th century dormer heads) and copying elements from elsewhere (the embedded gateway is from the Scots College in Paris). At the rear is a turret stair and decorated portal which survive from Provost Robertson's 16th century house, which stood on this site.

24 24-26 Upperkirkgate
1694 (restored)
The curious corbelled skews at the ends of the front with sundials may have terminated a wooden

superstructure, probably a balcony, as in Byron's house in Broad Street.

25 Schoolhill

Beyond George Street, Upperkirkgate becomes Schoolhill, which, until the construction of Rosemount Viaduct, stopped at the Denburn Valley. Schoolhill was straightened in the 1880s improvements to the city to secure a good wide route from the new Rosemount Viaduct to Broad Street. As a result, George Jameson's tall, turretted 16th century house was removed and replaced by a row of tenements by Matthews and Mackenzie (the only folly of Matthews' Provostship). Houses on the south side of the street (amongst them the celebrated Sang School), were also taken down then.

St Nicholas Centre

Thomson, Taylor, Craig and Donald, from 1967 Bridges the natural dip in Upperkirkgate to provide a two level shopping centre. The upper level (entered from Flourmill Lane, St Nicholas Churchyard or a truncated St Nicholas Street) has relatively few shops but much gardening and a jaunty bandstand. At the corner of the garden deck and the churchyard is John Smith's Grammar School Lodge removed here in the 1860s. Below, in what was St Nicholas Street, is enclosed shopping.

Above: Schoolhill in 1918.
Left: Jameson's House.

George Jameson (1588-1644) was born in Aberdeen and went to Antwerp to study art with the great Rubens alongside Van Dyck. On his return to Scotland he established a studio in Schoolhill and painted portraits. His own self portrait is in the nearby Art Gallery. At Woolmanhill at the old Playfield he made an enclosed, semi-public pleasure garden whose walls were ornamented by his own painting. He was in Edinburgh in the 1630s where he painted a portrait of Charles I. In 1634 he travelled to Italy and died in Edinburgh ten years later.
We have public parks and open spaces, palatial schools, and finer Churches wrote builder John Morgan, *but all this is poor compensation for a good deal of ruthless and wholesale destruction of many old and time honoured landmarks that can never be brought back. One of the most regrettable of these is what was known as Jameson's House in Schoolhill, a good example of Scotch turreted work: another was Mar's Lodgings near the top of the Gallowgate, others are the oak spire of the City Churches, and the old House of Rubislaw.*

27

Aberdeen City Library

RCAHMS

RCAHMS

I got access to the Churchyard by permission of Police Inspector Dey, known from his stature as the longest Dey, saw the flames enwrapping the wooden spire, and the lead running down it in molten streams, observed the clock hands drop to the bottom of the dial, heard the fall of Auld Lawrie, the historic bell, as it crashed to the bottom of the tower, and witnessed the collapse of the spire as it bowed towards the east and came plunging down in a cascade of fire. MacKinnon Recollections.

26 **St Nicholas Kirk**
From 12th century
Founded before 1151 St Nicholas, (known as the *Mither Kirk*) was the largest mediaeval Burgh Kirk in Scotland of which survive the late 12th century north transept, known as Collinson's aisle, and St Mary's Chapel — the groined vaulted crypt under the East Church beautifully built by Aberdeen's Master Mason Sir Andrew Wrycht in 1438 (restored sympathetically by Dr William Kelly, 1898). Not untypically in Scotland, St Nicholas was divided at the Reformation, and East St Nicholas was recased by Archibald Simpson when he *restored* it, 1835-1837, at which time, the remains of a very early choir — (shorter, narrower with a semi-circular apse) were uncovered. It was given a splendid chandelier called a **Sunlight** which consisted of a large number of gas jets placed in the ceiling under a reflector, cooled by water. In 1874, the water appears to have dried up; and East St Nicholas, and the marvellous early 16th century lead-covered spire, went up in flames. William Smith, son of John Smith, rebuilt both chancel and crossing between 1875 and 1877.

Aberdeen City Library

West St Nicholas

James Gibbs from 1741

The nave became the West Church at the Reformation, but fell into disrepair after the Glorious Revolution when many Aberdonians turned non-conformist and the congregation of the West Church followed its deposed minister to the Trinity Church near the Green. It was ruinous when occupied by the Duke of Cumberland's troops, on his way to Culloden. In 1741, a plain sober nave was designed by Aberdeen's famous architectural son James Gibbs, the architect of St Martin in the Fields, London, and many other celebrated buildings. Gibbs was made a Burgess in 1739: in gratitude he presented the design free of charge to the City. The Trustees delayed until sufficient income accrued for construction which was executed by James Wylie between 1752 and 1755 after Gibbs' death. Of smooth sandstone with crisp architectural ornament, its barrel vaulted interior has

Left: West St Nicholas drawn by Curtis Green.
Top: Nave.
Above: Hamilton Monument with William Smith's Spire.

Opposite, top to bottom:
St Nicholas in early 19th century.
St Mary's Chapel.
Collinson's Aisle.
St Nicholas on fire.

The east and west Churches are both very good. The magistrates sit in the West Church under a very superb canopy, and their seat is covered with crimson velvet adorned with a gold fringe. Alexander Carlyle, 1765.

St Nicholas The churches have been excellently repaired; and including its burial ground and handsome Facade of a railing along the street, it is a great honour to the place. Lord Cockburn, 1844.

contemporary pews, and a splendid Town's Loft used when the Council is *kirked*.

Open daily (except Tuesday) in the summer.

St Nicholas Churchyard is an oasis much frequented in good weather. There are many table tombs, and monuments attached to the inner walls of the Churchyard. There are also fine free standing monuments, such as John Smith's Hamilton Monument, 1843 — the perfect *aedicule*, on a specially high base, four ionic columns supporting entablature and roof, all to enclose a severely plain urn.

McKean

Back Wynd
St Nicholas is bounded on the west by Back Wynd, a short street of generally low, late 18th century buildings, although St Nicholas Kirk House (opposite the West Gate) is Victorian Palladian. Before the building of Union Street, Back Wynd led down to the Green, and was the last street on this side of the mediaeval town.

27 **James Dun's House**
61 Schoolhill, perhaps by William Law, 1769
Two-storey Georgian house built of mixed granite, home of the Rector of the Grammar School then just opposite, and now used as a museum. *Open daily 10 am-5 pm.*

There used to be a row of similar houses along the south side of Schoolhill. Dun's eastern neighbour was squashed under the rather baroque tenement now on the site, but yet another still *lives* inside Taylor's Art Salon. Others to the west were replaced in 1901 by J.

28 Ogg Allan **Old Central School,** full of imperial vigour with fine French detail (especially in the high pitched gables), and a large low dome at the corner — giving it a characteristic early 20th century profile.

The wide, irregular oblong space planted with trees on the north side is enclosed by phased civic and collegiate designs by Matthews and Mackenzie in pink and white granite. Pink was used for the characteristically flat architectural ornaments. **Gray's School of Art,** 1884, founded by John Gray, was followed shortly by its partner, the **Art Gallery** to the west. The corner block of mansion tenements, 54-70 Schoolhill, are also by Matthews and Mackenzie, 1886. Shirras Laing's (46-52 Schoolhill) in sympathy is by John Rust, 1897.

Brogden

Robert Gordon (1665-1732) was the son of an Aberdeen advocate and grandson of his famous namesake Sir Robert Gordon of Straloch, the cartographer; and a nephew of James Gordon of Rothiemay to whom we are indebted for much of our knowledge of Aberdeen and Edinburgh in the 17th century. He became a merchant trading with the Baltic port of Danzig (now Gdansk, Poland) where he acquired a fortune. Unmarried, his household in Aberdeen known for economy bordering on parsimony, he left his fortune for the founding of a Hospital for the education of the poor boys of Aberdeen.

Top: Back Wynd.
Above: James Dun's House.
Below: Robert Gordon's Group.

Brogden

29 **Robert Gordon's Hospital**
Begun by William Adam, from 1731
An archway guarded by a magnificent granite statue of Gordon of Khartoum frames the *Auld Hoose,* built for the education of poor boys of Aberdeen. William Adam's design was a two-storey block, flanked by pavilions with high bell-shaped pediments, the centre emphasised by a statue of Gordon by John Cheere, and a cupola above. Although complete by 1739 (from which date a good panelled room on the first floor survives) it was not occupied by pupils till 1750. Its grounds were sequestered by the Duke of Cumberland during 1745, who made an earthwork in the garden and dubbed it Fort Cumberland. John Smith remodelled and considerably extended the buildings, in 1833 adding the two strong advancing wings and the colonnades. The two blocks (1929-30) between the Schoolhill group and the Adam/Smith School are both

RCAHMS

by R. Leslie Rollo, sometime Head of the Aberdeen School of Architecture.

For the first century of its existence Robert Gordon's Hospital educated poor boys in conformity with its founder's wishes, although very generous benefactions in the early 19th century increased their number, and the size of the Hospital. In the 1880's 30 this all changed: Robert Gordon's College was created as an independent school on the public school model, and Gray's School of Art was established. Robert Gordon's College continues to thrive as such but Gray's grew over the years and took in various institutions of higher education outside the University, and was formally established as a Scottish Central Institution at the beginning of the 20th century. This is **Robert Gordon's Institute of Technology** the equivalent of a continental or American technical university. Thus the quadrangle is shared by Institute, College and Art Gallery.

31 **Art Gallery**

In 1905, Mackenzie added the top-lit Sculpture Court to the Art Gallery, to accompanying protests at *details more fitted for anatomical class-rooms which hinder rather than invite inspection and study.* The gallery is supported on an arcade of polished columns exemplifying the various colours of granite, then at the peak of its architectural and commercial importance. On an axis to the west is the austere War Memorial and Cowdray Hall, A. Marshall Mackenzie and Son, 1923-25, comparable to the best continental neo-classical work of the period. The quadrant colonnade at the south-west corner of the Schoolhill group (and facing into Union Terrace gardens) was meant to contain Edward VII's statue, but as it was built after the Great War it received instead a most noble stylized lion by William McMillan.

The Art Gallery is much patronised, and the Sculpture Court is a favourite meeting place. The main galleries are on the first floor and the Macdonald Collection of 19th century paintings, formed by granite merchant Alexander Macdonald of Kepplestone (advised by his friend Sir George Reid whose own paintings can be seen), hangs in two rooms which are still as they were finished by A. Marshall Mackenzie. The rest of the galleries have been altered to suit changing requirements and are both cheerful and efficient. There are paintings by Aberdeen artists George Jameson, William Dyce and James Giles, and 20th century artists are strongly represented.

The ground floor galleries contain sculpture, again largely 20th century, and local silver and glassware. There is also a small gallery named after James McBey. The Mackenzies' sober war memorial and the Cowdray Hall open from the Art Gallery. There is a good shop, and coffee shop. *Open from 10-5 daily, including Saturday. 2-5 Sunday.*

Above left: Robert Gordon's Hospital.
Below: Robert Gordon's Institute of Technology.
Bottom: Cowdray Hall and Art Gallery.

Brogden

Brogden

Aberdeen City Library

Aberdeen City Library

Top: James Giles' drawing of Simpson's masterpiece, the Triple Kirks.
Above: Simpson's alternative design with Union Bridge and Gardens, 1843.

Opposite, top: 37 Belmont Street.
Below left: St Nicholas Congregational Church.
Right: Belmont Street.

Triple Kirks

32 Archibald Simpson, 1843

I was much struck with the view from the bridge down towards the Infirmary wrote Lord Cockburn in 1844 *of a rude Cathedral looking mass which contains three Free Churches.*

East, West and South Churches, despite the ecclesiastical absurdity to speak of a Cathedral of the Disruption, form just such an impression. They commemorate the conflict between Church government and spiritual independence which, in 1843, impelled the two powerful ministers of the east and west parishes (occupying the chancel and the nave of St Nicholas) and their brother from the recently finished South Church to quit their ministries, taking large parts of their congregations with them. A large site, recently abandoned as a factory, was bought for the Free Congregations at the west end of Schoolhill — just in time: as the agent for Free's left the seller's office, he met an Establishment foe on his way to buy the site in spite!

It is fortunate for architecture in Aberdeen that the Free's agent succeeded, for the site and Simpson's response to it is the essence of the Triple Kirk's power. One Church faces north, a second east, with the third continuing its lofty prominence when viewed from the new districts to the west. The graceful brick spire (remarkably similar to one of the spires of the Elizabeth Kirche in Marburg), paid homage to the spire of old St Nicholas.

The West Kirk, and a very fractious and acquisitive lot they appear to have been, became upset when the railway invaded the Denburn, securing compensation for the *undermining* of their Church. With the proceeds, they built the handsome Langstane Kirk in Union Street. Their fears proved specious and most quickly returned, buying back their *old* Church from the railway company — at a profit, of course! That began an unhappy myth that the Triple Kirks are unsound and cheaply built, which various interested parties have used to their advantage in recent years.

After de-consecration in 1969, the old east part became a restaurant in 1974, named Simpsons after its architect. The western two thirds have been sadly and shamefully neglected, yet still stand with Simpson's spire soaring above oblivious: it has a stout granite heart within its brick skin, after all.

33 **Belmont Street**

Until the 1770s Belmont Street was an open pasture, after which it was quickly built up, now presenting a specially agreeable and varied scene. The earliest building was **No. 37**, the handsome 1788 Town House of Menzies of Pitfodels (his venerable old Lodging in the Castlegate soon to give way to Burn's new Bank): a five bay, two-storey, regular Georgian box, raised up half a floor, and ornamented by quoins and a good stone cornice. Originally a pair of pavilions flanked either side, the southern one charmingly recalled by an early 20th century shop. Immediately next door is William Leslie's
34 idiosyncratic **Congregational Church** of 1865, perhaps designed by the young James Souttar then working in Stockholm (for the apse is based on Lund Cathedral). It, and much else in Belmont Street, is even more effective from the south-west. There follows, on both sides of the street, low, late 18th century buildings.

William Leslie (1802-1879) was a builder and granite merchant who took a keen interest in architecture. He was agent for the Duke of Sutherland from 1836 and in 1844 began to build Dunrobin Castle and much else in the north. Sir Charles Barry was Dunrobin's architect but as he put it himself *The Duke has increased the size and accommodation of the Castle in the grand and picturesque style of architecture particular to Scottish Castles . . . and has succeeded very tolerably in carrying out that style from plans proposed by Mr Leslie of Aberdeen, modified both by the Duke and myself.*

Leslie was for long credited with the design of St Nicholas Congregational Church in Belmont Street but it now appears that the young James Souttar, then in Stockholm may have provided the design.

South Church, Belmont Street.

35 **South Church**
John Smith, 1830
Now known as St Nicholas West Kirk House, the
Church makes an interesting comparison with
Simpson's perpendicular St Andrew's Cathedral, King
Street. The South Church is lighter, almost Gothick,
in the whimsical 18th century fashion. This is
possibly a result of his use of granite, and has much to
do with the building's comparative isolation, and
movement of the facade. The tower, and black painted
clock faces, make it something of a landmark.

36 **Town School**, Little Belmont Street
John Smith, 1840
The school consists of an extremely severe portico of
plain doric columns, flanked by short wings and
pavilions: a very small, very monumental building
(more characteristic of Simpson's buildings and
unusual for Smith). When clean the building appears
almost to be made of one piece of stone.
    Next door (towards St Nicholas) is Cameron's Inn
(familarly **Ma Cameron's**), a favourite pub for
various ages, and one of considerable character: tiny
bars with old linings, old prints of Aberdeen and an
open fire.
    A jovial, tall Edwardian block of *chambers* marks the
old end of Belmont Street. To the left was the way to
the Green by Gaelic Lane (named for the late 18th
century Chapel for Highlandmen) and Back Wynd,
while **Patagonian Court** opens to the west through
an arch, and leads down steps to the Denburn (since
1859 in a culvert). This apparent detour illustrates
best the old pattern of the city, the topographical
problem to be overcome in changing that pattern, and
the key to the solution — Union Bridge.

Below: Patagonian Court.
Right: Town School.

Union Bridge
Thomas Fletcher and others, 1801
Work began on David Hamilton's winning design for a new bridge in 1801, but within a year the contractors found they had badly miscalculated and, with the Trustees' consent, withdrew. Thomas Fletcher, the Superintendent, also discovered that Hamilton's levels were in error. A new design was required, and John Rennie, still at work on the Aberdeenshire Canal, was consulted. Rennie gave in three schemes, one of which included a cast iron arch of 36 metres. Fletcher, who by this time knew the minds of the Trustees and the depth of their collective pocket, submitted a design for a single stone eliptical arch of 40 metres. Thomas Telford, consulted about that scheme, suggested a shallower roadway, and a batter to the end of piers. Those, with James Burn's design for the parapet, were added. It was completed in 1805, three years and three years' interest charges late, but otherwise to everybody's satisfaction. The Trustees and all the engineers had agreed that the Street should be made wider by 3.5 metres and the Bridge should be that much narrower — 12 metres wide instead of 15 because they saw it as a *Bridge* and wanted a handsome one. A hundred years later, however, it was seen rather as a tiresomely congested *Street*. It was therefore widened, and William Dyack's light steel arch is apparent from the bottom of the Patagonian Court.

Union Bridge in 1840. The Denburn still flows in the open, and the crowded factories near the Green can be seen. Smith's Trinity Hall has not yet been built.

Right: Windmill Brae, the old
entrance to Aberdeen.
Below: Correction Wynd from
Union Street.

Opposite, right: Correction
Wynd.
Below: Benholm's Lodging in its
original setting, drawn by J. C.
Nattes in 1799. *The view is
extremely picturesque and not unlike
some of the towns in Italy, in which
the style and masses of the building
to the north are often very similar.*

Aberdeen University Library

Old Highway
It is still possible to follow the Denburn Road under
Union Bridge to the Green, although the grisly
underside of the Trinity Shopping Centre makes this
somewhat less than inviting. Persevere. As the road
turns left (eastwards) steps rise westward (often
insalubrious, apparently not yet on the list of the
otherwise good Cleansing Department). This is the
tenuous remnant of the Old Highway, on the site of
Bow Brig, which until Union Bridge replaced it was
the way into Aberdeen. It connects (through a parking
garage!) to Windmill Brae and thus to the Hardgate.

37 The Green
The most ancient part of Aberdeen, the market place
long before it was moved up to the Castlegate, and the
presumed *centre* of the first settlement in the Dark
Ages. After 1500 years or so, nothing remains,
although the pattern of the Green and some nearby
streets is probably mediaeval. Some 12th century
monastic graves have been discovered some distance
south towards Guild Street, but no surviving buildings
predate the turn of the 18th and 19th centuries, when
it had become one of the industrial sections of
Aberdeen. Hadden's factory, and Ley's and Masson's
factory, both great employers in the linen manufacture
were located nearby. The Green's current sad and
neglected appearance may partly be due to this; but is
more the result of planning stalemate which can be
seen at its most vicious in the south-east corner. The
large multiple stores up on Union Street want to
expand southwards and smother this part of the city,
in the way the Trinity Centre and Littlewoods have
already done. This has been resisted locally, and the
result is plain to see.

It is possible (for the adventurous), to proceed along
East Green and *under* Market Street and Union Street
to the Netherkirkgate, by Carnegie's Brae, another
ancient way into the heart of Aberdeen, from which
the vaults under Market Street and Union Street can
be easily seen.

Livesley

38 Correction Wynd

So named because from the 17th century it lead to a House of Correction. The Wynd passes under Union Street and beside St Nicholas Churchyard. The buildings here are mostly 19th century, and of no particular interest individually. **Owlies**, no 12 Correction Wynd was imaginatively remade by E. G. Smith, 1980, into a restaurant, specially attractive in the afternoon. The sculpture, Owlie, is by Helen Dennerley.

As Correction Wynd turns by St Nicholas (St Mary's Chapel entrance is at the left) it originally became the Netherkirkgate, and although this old street is partly covered by Marks and Spencer, it shows up around the corner where Carnegie's Brae comes from *underground* to join it. At this point stood Benholm's Lodging until removed in 1962. Netherkirkgate leads past Flourmill Lane and St

39 Katherine's Lane to Broad Street opposite. **Concert Court**, the only court to survive, contains the Advocate's Hall, by James Matthews, 1869. Of no particular interest externally, the surprise is the splendid decoration inside, especially the stencilled walls by Daniel Cottier. The main room was restored as an extra High Court Room (PSA, 1984) and the Advocate's Library above is also notable.

Livesley

Aberdeen University Library

37

Brogden

Union Street looking west from the Castlegate.

Union Street
From 1801

One of the finest streets in the Empire . . . about a mile long, straight elegantly edificed, well-gemmed with public buildings. Imperial Gazetteer, 1865.

Union Street offers an unparalleled opportunity to appreciate the variety of consistently good architecture, designed over a century and a half by a number of outstanding architects, within an overall consistency. The common elements to notice are the division of each building into a base (the ground floor) the principal facade above (often with columns) terminated by a cornice line, an attic above that, and the roof. Most variety in detail occurs around the doors, the windows, and the cornice.

Early progress in the creation of Union Street had been hampered by doubts about the project, difficulties of building, and not least by the city's bankruptcy in 1817. For the project to succeed, the stances on either side of the street (causeway) had to be bid for, and taken up timeously. The major building works of the bridge and causeways had to proceed expeditiously, and difficulties of ownership, and questions of compensation had to be sorted out speedily. Nothing happened when it should have, and, as interest had to be paid on the moneys financing the works anyway, the interest soon overbalanced income. Nowadays cost and time overruns on capital projects have their own solutions and terminology: in early 19th century Aberdeen it was known as bankruptcy.

Further Trustees were appointed in 1817. It was then thought that the city would lose £80,000 absolutely. Fortunately, the temptation to accept cheaper building in order to speed up the taking up of stances was resisted and within a few years, matters were resolved.

40 **Union Buildings**
Archibald Simpson, from 1819
Union Buildings sets the standard by which the rest of
this great street is to be judged. It began with **No. 19**,
Baillie Galen's House, built of smooth ashlar white
granite, an arcaded ground floor separated by a string
course from the upper two floors. The facade is
unrelieved apart from its well proportioned windows,
cill course at third-floor windows, a projecting cornice
and short parapet. (The visible roof is modern: the
original would not have been seen.)

In 1822 Simspon added a much larger section to the
east (the joint is clear at the east end of Baillie Galen's
House) forming a coherent terrace whose central
section consists of five further bays of the same
design, stepped forward slightly and terminated by a
long wall head panel. A further three bays at the east
end, balancing Baillie Galen's original, also face into
the Castlegate, for which Simpson created a quite
different facade, transforming the plain wall and
windows with four gigantic Ionic columns and three
huge windows ornamented at the eaves line by another
wallhead panel. The lofty room thus indicated was
created for the **Atheneum**, a *Library* where the
newspapers could be read, an excellent place for
meetings. Latterly it became Jimmy Hay's, a
restaurant famous from the 19th century to its tragic
loss in 1973 when the whole building was burnt out.
Union Buildings was rebuilt by Thomson Taylor
Craig and Donald, but the great room, alas, became
two floors of offices.

Top: Simpson's design for Union
Buildings.
Above: Union Buildings.

41 **40-44 Union Street**
Archibald Simpson, 1811
The first to be built in the street, it was designed
while Simpson was still employed in David Laing's
office in London for John Morrison of Auchintoul. It
is a young man's building — all exuberance and
complexity. His monumental and classical reticence
was yet to come. The double-height principal room
(with pilasters and segmental arches) at the ground
level, is in the *middle* of the building, with entrance at
the east side (with arched tops and corinthian
columns) bearing a block-like balcony at the first floor
level. Above the arched lower floors is a regular group
of framed windows, then a modillion cornice and low
attic. An identical entrance on the west side leads to a
second house, two thirds of which is extremely plain!
Buildings on the south side followed in 1812 near
Putachieside. Nos. 57-65 Union Street, soon to
become the **Royal Hotel**, were visited by Lord
Cockburn in 1853: *We had a beastly Circuit on a
sanded floor, and came away eagerly this morning from
the stinking Royal Hotel.* Later in the century, an extra

40-44 Union Street.

Adelphi

Dr William Kelly (1861-1944) was a scholar-architect, a pupil and successor to William Smith. A great and observant traveller as his sketch books attest, Kelly made his Grand Tour in 1885 before entering partnership with Smith. His work for the Trustees of Aberdeen Savings Bank brought an early masterpiece, their Head Office at 19 Union Terrace (1893-96). Equally characteristic, however, was his more self-effacing work: for Aberdeen Royal Infirmary from the 1880s until his retirement in 1928; as consultant to the Cowdrays at Dunecht; and specially his work in Old Aberdeen, repairs and restoration of such mastery and delicacy that they might go quite unnoticed. Yet Kelly never quite unnoticed — a big man, he was such a stickler for good workmanship that apprentices and workmen went in fear and trembling.

Opposite, top: Simpson's design for Market Street.
Below: Old Post Office by Simpson, 1842.

floor of steeply pitched, rather gothic, dormers were added by Dr William Kelly when these buildings were
42 turned into Royal Galleries department store, now Fraser's and recently completely refurbished. The stretch between here and Union Buildings was completed in the early 1820s, and survive in that form (apart from the delightfully bumptious 39-45 Union Street, William Smith, 1877).

43 **Adelphi**, 1815
Adelphi Court, now known simply as the Adelphi is all that remains of the ancient St Katherine's Hill: a short street, with an even shorter leg at the end. Some of the buildings are granite rubble and are harled leaving the doors and windows picked out with crisp granite margins. It has an unexpected, rather old world charm.

Esslemont and Macintosh, Aberdeen's grandest old department store (26-30 Union Street, Ellis and Wilson) is part-classical, but loaded with Netherlandish detail; around the windows, at the roof line, at the corners and specially noticeable in the heavy doric frieze. The west block, **no. 32-38** by R. G. Wilson, 1897 is all gables and oriel windows with a decided vertical emphasis. St Katherine's Lane joins the old Netherkirkgate to Union Street between those two buildings, and something of the mediaeval scale and jumble can be appreciated still.

Union Chambers
James Henderson, 1895
An undeniably handsome replacement of Simpson's original five bay composition, similar to the Bank of Scotland in Castle Street. It has a curious attic storey which terminates in a pair of wall head chimneys. The ground floor mixture of shop windows, and entrances to the Chambers above, is original.

44 **Clydesdale Bank** (60-62 Union Street)
James Matthews, 1862-63
By far the richest building in lower Union Street. The bold detailing of the dentil cornice (which breaks forward 8 times on the Union Street front) with little shell decorations on top; the channelled masonry, the giant corinthian pilasters in the centre; the triplet arched windows (outlined in pink granite, just so we should not miss them!) and the varied blocks, urns and chimneys of the top floor, all spell architectural opulence. Its interior is equally splendid.

45 **Market Street**
Archibald Simpson, 1840
Constructed both to obscure the miserable sight of Putachieside, and to provide a connection between

Aberdeen City Library

Union Street and the harbour. 67 and 73-79 Union Street were of Simpson's standard type, except the arcaded ground floor was actually an arcade. Immediately south were two one-storey buildings, the western one still surviving as Knowles Greengrocers, although its shallow pilasters and bays have been cut by later shop windows. The eastern block recently perished along with Simpson's fine Post Office (the third) of 1842 to make way for the granite-faced Fraser's Department Store, 1985 by Hugh Martin which carried on the arcade theme and adds canted bay windows to it.

The **New Market**, 1840-42 (Archibald Simpson) turned the ancient Green into an enormous covered market: over 100 metres long it had an arcade with an extra row of shops overlooking the vast interior space. The show front to market Street was simplified and slab-like. It was burnt out in 1882, rebuilt and regretably, in 1971 replaced by Robert Matthew, Johnson-Marshall and Partners, as an extended British Home Stores, with the Market confined to the two lower floors.

46 **Mechanics Institute** (now the Bon Accord Hotel) Archibald Simpson (with William Ramage), 1845 Its deep black-painted frieze and cornice and the tall first floor have a handsome aspect, especially from Hadden Street (the east branch of the Green). Two further palace blocks are worthy of note: the former **Union Club** at 18-22 Market Street by James Matthews and, opposite, the Royal Bank (originally a City of Glasgow Bank) 1858, by William Smith.

Simpson's corner blocks have both disappeared; 67 Union Street was reconstructed in similar style later in the 19th century, and itself was under threat until the

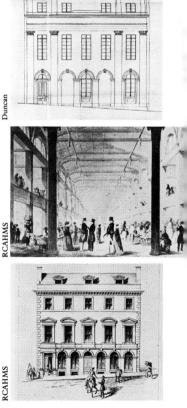

Duncan

RCAHMS

RCAHMS

Above: New Market interior.
Below: 18-22 Market Street.

78-80 Union Street.

Brogden

Scottish Georgian Society and others persuaded Frasers to incorporate it into their new store. The western corner block was replaced in 1929 by George Watt in a marvellous cross between advanced Greek revival (*note* acroteria and very shallow pediment) and art deco, especially in the design of the steel windows. It might be the obvious candidate for the last classical 47 building in Union Street if it were not for the hot competition put up by **The Royal Bank of Scotland**, 78-80 Union Street, 1936 by Jenkins and Marr. This cubic mass of building is lightened by the glass and metal openings between the colossal corinthian columns. A heavy cornice separates third and fourth floors where the panels between the windows make a delicate contrast. The heavily framed end doorways, and the sharply decorated central one add interest.

The junction of St Nicholas Street and Union Street was always called *The Queen* because, until 1964 when she was banished to Queen's Cross, it was ornamented by the statue of Victoria in old age. The small gap over Carnegie's Brae was bridged at that time so as to make a suitable entrance to Marks and Spencers' new store (Munro and Partners, 1964, recently extended), a block resplendent in polished granite. To get this site, Marks and Spencer moved and re-erected at Tillydrone the 16th century Benholm's Lodging (better known as the Wallace Tower, see p. 126).

Gloucester Hotel, c. 1824
82-106 Union Street is created from four individual blocks all built before 1824, to the typical pattern, the hotel on the upper floors (linked by a bridge to a further block in Correction Wynd) with shops at ground floor. Opposite are two wider blocks (five bays) probably by Archibald Simpson, 1830, with block pediment and chimney stacks as a feature. Then follows a typical Union Street block of about 1830.

St Nicholas Centre looking to Market Street.

Livesley

The first floor of Woolworths is a curiosity — three large arched openings and a supporting bay to the east, but none to the west, with rather flat but rich architectural ornamentation: this 1900 insertion by Robert Wilson was, happily, unique.

48 **Facade**, St Nicholas Churchyard
John Smith, 1829
This colonnade carries Union Street on as a terrace while making a fitting entry to St Nicholas. Based on Decimus Burton's recently completed Screen at Hyde Park Corner, it has original iron work.

Smith's *Facade* with Queen's Cinema.

Albert Duguid

49 **Queen's Cinema** (originally Advocate's Hall)
John Smith, 1836
Built in a style which suggests that Smith looked on this part of Union Street as a sort of architectural crescendo. Back Wynd facade has a pediment over the central feature, the enrichments to the curving corner section and the Union Street front remodelled by A. Marshall Mackenzie in 1898.

50 **124-132 Union Street** (north side) are both c. 1820 by Simpson, as are probably nos. 136-144, for it has his block pediments and chimneys on two fronts. When viewed from Union Bridge or Union Terrace, a seemingly typical Aberdeen block is revealed to be doubled with a further four storeys of rusticated stone carried in three great arches with square-headed windows picking up the rhythm from the upper section.

51 **Trinity Hall** (Littlewoods)
John Smith and William Smith, 1846
Perhaps because the Seven Incorporated Trades longed to underline their links to late mediaeval times, or because the Smiths were infected with the romance of the Middle Ages, Trinity Hall was the first

The Churchyard was extended considerably, in the year 1819, by the purchase of the piece of ground running from the Correction to the Back Wynd and about forty yards in breadth from Union Street. In the year 1829 plans were prepared by John Smith, City Architect, for a handsome front to the Churchyard and for an entrance into it. The plan adopted was the present Facade. Formerly this piece of ground was generally used by itinerating exhibitions — *the wild beasts*, jugglers, fire-eaters, swings, merry-go-rounds, giants, dwarfs and peep-shows. Two great institutions of this nature used to be frequent visitors to the city — the one Wombwell's Menagerie and the other *Cocker's Show*, which had the *horse of knowledge, the learned pig* etc.

building in Union Street to dress itself historically. It is elegantly Tudor, mostly turrets, pointed arches with tracery and shaped tabling over the windows. The Hall with its *mediaeval* hammerbeam roof, was restored by Littlewoods, in response to local pressure, and converted into a restaurant. The excellent and important collection of early furniture, and the stained glass have been removed to a new Trinity Hall.

C & A, Union Bridge
North and Partners, 1956
A replacement of the Palace Hotel which had been burnt during the Second World War, C & A's is a plain granite clad block of five storeys (the top one masquerades as a roof). Each front suggests kinship with its union Street neighbours by the subtle grouping of windows into bays of threes and sixes.

RCAHMS

Livesley

Top: Old Trinity Hall, retained in Littlewoods as a restaurant.
Above: View from Union Bridge.

View from Union Bridge
From Union Bridge to the north is the finest panorama of Aberdeen architecture. Mostly conscious, partly accidental, architects and their clients contributed over more than a hundred years to this civic design. From west to east the buildings are A.

52 Marshall Mackenzie's **Commercial Union** Insurance Building, known locally as the *Monkey House*, whose Doric porch at the corner is still a favoured meeting
53 place. **Lloyds Bank**, 1979, by Jenkins and Marr is an attempt at *contextual* design — thin granite hung on steel frame, with bay windows recalling their neighbours to the north. Mackenzie's **Caledonian**
54 **Hotel**, fussily asymmetrical, is followed by several surviving town houses of the early 19th century, and then Dr William Kelly's superb **Trustee Savings**
55 **Bank** of 1896, a tall, crisp palazzo of white granite with razor sharp arrises — the fine detail attributable to the fear that Kelly's workmen and apprentices had of him. This is followed by no less than three palazzo blocks, (two of 1887 and 1896, by Marshall
56 Mackenzie's firm, and one of 1906 by A. G. Sidney Mitchell and Wilson) for the **County Offices**.
For all their diversity, these buildings read as a Terrace, enhanced by their common material, the

mature trees of Corbiehaugh and by Marshall
Mackenzie's balustrade, carried on eliptical arches —
one of which is the old Bow Brig.

The view is closed by Viaducts as they partly bridge
the Denburn, and are partly embanked within Union
Terrace gardens. William Wallace's statue (1888,
W. Grant Stevenson) stands guard in front of three
buildings — representing in turn *Education, Salvation*
57 and *Damnation*. The **Central Library**, an irregular
and rather romantic composition on Renaissance
sources; the original eastern part was symmetrically
58 designed by George Watt, and won in competition in
1891. Marshall Mackenzie's **St Mark's Church**,
1892, is basically a parish kirk, given civic prominence
by the addition of the giant corinthian portico, and the
high dome on glazed drum above. Frank Matcham's
59 **His Majesty's Theatre** 1904-08 is typical of his
work, although its setting at the far end of the
gardens, and its white granite make it special.
Matcham was a celebrated music-hall architect and the
recently restored interior of this Majesty's is a banquet
of Edwardian exuberance.

Top: Union Terrace.
Above: *Education, Salvation and
Damnation.*
Left: Woolmanhill.
Below: One of Kelly's Cats.

Peeping round from behind this group are
60 Archibald Simpson's **Royal Infirmary** at
Woolmanhill, a sublimely neo-classical block with a
wide central pediment, set back in wooded grounds.
In the far distance, a master stroke (in compositional
terms) is the tall, castellated red brick barrier of the
61 **Broadford Works** appearing as if it were a mediaeval
town wall.

In the north-east corner is the **Cowdray Hall**. The
eastern flank begins, indeed in a sense the whole
composition pivots on, Archibald Simpson's **Triple
Kirks**. That their picturesque quality was in the
architect's mind, is attested by their romantic
appearance over his shoulder in his portrait by James
Giles.

The back of Belmont Street is naturally picturesque
with small scale buildings stepping down the slope to
the Denburn, enhanced by Ellis and Wilson's **Trades
62 Hall** (behind No. 47), receding (as it were) from the
Triple Kirks and the **Congregational Church.**

45

Commercial Union with Kelly's parapet and King Edward.

Assembly Rooms and Union Street looking east.

Commercial Union, 146 Union Street
Undeniably splendid with channeled masonry, Doric porch, and little pediments over the windows on the ground floor. The columns above, the frieze, and the reverse consoles linking the attic are also worth noting.

148 and **150 Union Street** are both fairly early 1820s: 150 with a ground floor, which looks like the best pattern from the early 19th century, really the 1956 product of A. G. R. Mackenzie's imagination.

Apart from the late 19th century re-working of **167-169 Union Street**, the block between the Bridge and Ellis and Wilson's Bank of Scotland (1893) is of the 1820s.

154 and **158 Union Street** are intruders in a terrace otherwise of the 1820s. Offices (or chambers), hence the large areas of glass in canted bays with pairs of double flats above, liberally endowed with obelisks, shaped gablets, and outsized voussoirs. 158 is a bit more chaste.

63 **Assembly Rooms**
Archibald Simpson, 1820
The Building of the Assembly Rooms was another act of faith. It provided grander and more refined accommodation than the New Inn or the Lemon Tree in Huxter Row, and was intended as a place in which country gentry and town gentry could decently mingle. There is a giant ionic porch to Union Street, ample enough itself for reception, or lingering goodnights after a party. The main rooms inside are a

46

Music Hall in its original state.

Assembly Rooms, interior.

Ballroom (now remade as cloakrooms and lavatories despite having been saved from such a fate at a Public Enquiry), a broad central corridor and on the west side a card room and a circular supper room. Rooms for billiards were, discreetly, upstairs. In 1858 James Matthews completed the project by adding the **Music Hall** to the north end (in Golden Square).

A relatively perfect terrace c. 1830 of four houses stands opposite the Assembly Rooms and Music Hall. 64 **213 Union Street** is a decidedly splendid drinking shop refitted by Jenkins and Marr in the 1930s. Its frontage is very sober — bronze panels and discreetly frosted glass. Inside all is equally severe. The shallow vault of the ceiling has robust late 17th century style plaster work and leather covered banquettes line one side, while opposite across the black and white marble floor, is a long mahogany bar, with rather baroque ornamentation behind. There used to be loyal (black and white) photographs of the Sovereign and the Duke of Edinburgh.

221 Union Street, 1830s, was refitted as part of Watt and Grants Store, and the roof raised to form a genteel coffee and luncheon room. This is all gone, replaced by offices.

47

My father erected the fine block known popularly as MacKinnon's buildings, from which the clan crest of a boar's head still looks down on Union Street. For the new building my father proposed to employ his brother-in-law, the City Architect, who submitted a plan, which showed it to be supported by massive pillars of masonry, the aggregate width of which would encroach substantially on the intended shop fronts. My father objected, and suggested, in order to get the best results by way of rent, that the building should be supported on iron pillars and beams as is invariably done today, so as to leave all possible frontage available for shop windows. But the architect, who may have been right from an aesthetic point of view, refused to adopt this method, and said in my hearing that he "was not going to prostitute his profession for anybody". MacKinnon, Recollections.

Langstane Kirk.

Robert McAllister

Opposite:
Above: Union Street West in 19th century.
Below: Scott Sutherland's 250-252 Union Street.

65 **225-363 Union Street**
Late 19th century
An imperial-scale blocks of chambers, which respect the nature of Union Street, taking their eaves line from nos. 267-271 of the 1830s, although looking forward to a new century. This is specially so of A. Marshall Mackenzie's 245-257 Union Street, MacKinnon's Buildings, a tall group which closes the view from Huntly Street, with a lively skyline (it rises to a high central section) facade of canted bays, and doubled windows.

66 **208-210 Union Street**
George Bennett Mitchell, 1911
A somewhat scaled down version of the Commercial Union block, with much richer modelling, especially the octagonal tower and dome. But the rest of this section is positively neurotic. **212-228** are c. 1840, sharing a common cornice line. But above that cornice almost anything can happen! **212-216** Union Street have grown shaped gables, and curly wallheads. **220** has grown another three floors, and rusticated ones at that, with handsome balustrade, and central stone fronted dormer. **222-224** and **226-228** have retained their 1840s sobriety — indeed they have the only surviving sunken area in Union Street, and original front at ground floor.

67 At **6 Union Row** is an interesting small classical composition of 1927 by Jenkins and Marr and there is a later and ingenious *dormer conversion*. At the end stands the entrance to **Grampian House**, a speculative office building of pleasing neighbourliness, by Cunningham Glass Partnership, 1983-84.

68 **Langstane Kirk**
James Matthews, 1869
The west end of Union Street is enlivened (from as far east as the Castlegate) by the two spires, which help close the vista. Langstane, properly the West Church of St Andrew, is ecclesiological Gothic with a vast galleried nave. It is set back from the street, forming a small, but very lively public *square*, very often the scene of the Church's own good works. The Congregations who had quit the *Mither Kirk* with great sadness often wished to be buried there, and their fondness for it is attested to by spires in imitation of the original: the taller and skinnier the better. The Langstane Kirk has three tall parts, and then the spire — ornamented by four pinnacles at the corners, a gablet to each side, plus four gothic aedicules in the lower edges of the spire. As these are normally seen at an angle, they add a touch of lightness.

Aberdeen City Library

69 Gilcomston South (Free) Church
William Smith, 1868

This congregation came from Gilcomston Parish Church at the north end of Summer Street, and for many years were housed in a modest, classical Church building in Huntly Street, opposite the Blind Asylum. Fiery preaching attracted great numbers, and this church was built as their new home. Its great nave is supported by three gabled sections to the west which step back with the line of the street, whereas the bell tower and spire step forward, and appear detached. Add to this a balancing short tower at the southeast corner and the result is picturesque. One of architecture's happier accidents was the removal of decayed sandstone from the bell stage of the main tower: it contributes a sculptural aspect to the building's other qualities.

248 Union Street is the last house to be built, 1869, although its design derives from the 1830s. **250-252 Union Street** by T. Scott Sutherland is art deco in style of c. 1933. **260 Union Street**, part of a terrace of c. 1830, two-storey, three window houses with continuous cornices, with altered ground floor levels. **335-369 Union Street**, c. 1830, are identical, with the exception of the added details of the doorway of 339.

373-377 Union Street, John Rust, 1901, is at pains to carry through the cornice line of its eastern neighbour, yet swells out into two canted bays before being carried on as a band course in the next pair of buildings.

The self-contained Union Street dwelling house of these days (1860s) was substantial, well designed and comfortable, with ample entrance hall and staircase and spacious rooms. The decoration and furnishings might run to green and gold wall-papers, drop crystal chandeliers, and other embellishments considered very beautiful. . . . There was no bathroom in my father's house, and the domestic servants' quarters were dark and limited. There was no hot water in the kitchen, and no cold water above the first floor. Strange to say there was no sewer, and in our house the sewage passed into two cesspools in the sunk area at the rear and immediately under the back windows. These cesspools were closed by unsealed flagstones to which iron rungs were attached for lifting them, and we, the children, used to raise them out of ill-directed curiosity.
MacKinnon, *Recollections*

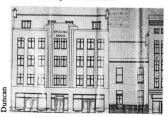

Duncan

381-399 Union Street.

381-389 Union Street (Habitat and Michies) are in the style of Simpson, the western end returned resolutely with a block pediment and smartly detailed chimney stack, as if it were the end house. Yet
71 **393-399,** the Halifax Building Society, c. 1830, and thought to be by John Smith, was already built. It has two-storey pilaster strips and both ends are canted (the frontage was advanced by a metre in the late 19th century) and was obviously, if curiously, intended to stand clear.

72 **Union Place**, c. 1820s
The final section of Union Street was originally known as Union Place. It is slightly narrower than the rest of the street, and earlier, being mostly built up in the 1820s. There was a settlement here already, along Summer Street (which used to lead to Gilcomston Parish Church, now Denburn Parish Church — itself at first a Chapel of Ease) where the buildings are much smaller, like **402-422 Union Street**. Most of Union Place was made up of two-storey, generally three window houses. An exception is **No. 421**, a three-storey building with a Venetian window off centre in the first floor. Union Place lacks the sense of cohesion of the rest of Union Street and appears less stern and neo-classical. It has an independent life as a shopping area (almost suburban) although this is becoming obscured by larger shops moving westward.

Capitol Cinema.

73 **Capitol Cinema**
A. Marshall Mackenzie and Son and George (John Marr and David Stokes), 1932-34
Both a picture palace, and a restatement of Union Street civic architecture in '30s dress. The cinema part has three tall windows to Union Street above the canopy (these light the refreshment room which retains its original light fittings and furniture, and some (at least) of the original carpet. Above the windows are small panels of sculpture, and the cinema is finished off with an *art-deco* pediment.

74 **478-484 Union Street**
John Smith, 1830
Originally constructed as the Town's Cistern, twice as tall as its (original) neighbours, this great tank pretended to be a tenement: in 1900 it was converted to just that.

75 **Christ's College**
Thomas Mackenzie, 1850
Union Street is terminated by this picturesque composition. It was a foundation to train ministers for the Free Church and is an essay in Tudor forms, the

Aberdeen City Library

tower to the rear imparting a castle-quality that makes its historicism a bit more local. Across the street in Alford Place is a row of granite cottages of which two are specially notable. No. 3 (Davidson and Kays) has an interesting new front of 1968 by Mackie Ramsay and Taylor.

Christ's College Library, 2 Alford Place
A. Marshall Mackenzie (then of Matthews and Mackenzie), 1887
An original cottage has been cunningly remodelled inside to provide a two-storey Porter's house to the left, and a students' hall to the right, the street frontage given dormers with elaborate bargeboards. The real surprise is inside: a long library, added to the north in the garden, with a wagon vaulted wooden roof with clerestory windows at the end in imitation of King's College Chapel.

St James's Episcopal Church
Arthur Clyne from 1887
Of pink granite and set back from the Union Street frontage, it is curiously easy to miss from the east. Handsome rose window but still lacking its bellstage and spire.

Thomas Mackenzie's Christ's College forms a picturesque termination to Union Street. A similar termination was proposed for the east end in 1850 by John Gibb, below, but it was nearly half a century before it was realised by James Souttar as the Salvation Army Citadel.

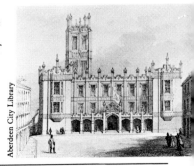

Aberdeen City Library

NEO CLASSICAL TOWN

There were several parallels with the Capital. James Young's competition entry for the New Street and Bridge recalls Robert Adam's Charlotte Square, 1791, in two enormous terraces, stretching from Castlegate to the Denburn with a nine bay pedimented centre, enlivened by terminal pavilions (Simpson's Aberdeen Hotel derives from the north western one) and simple advancing triplets of bays halfway along each very long *wing*. The bridging between the *old* town and the *new* town in Edinburgh is repeated in Aberdeen, and to some extent the inherent contrast between the two (which it took Edinburgh half a century fully to appreciate) is also apparent in Aberdeen. The treatment of the Denburn Valley with its *originally* canalized Denburn recalls the treatment of the North Loch before the coming of the railway. Even the creation of a public garden between the two halves occurred in both cities.

For all their similarities of site and intention, Aberdeen did not become a second Edinburgh. A grand bridge, and even grander causeway leading to it (with all the buildings it presupposed) was one thing: it was quite another to build a large new city on the fields to the west. And yet schemes for large and regular layouts continued in Aberdeen until the 1840s.

From the earliest days of Union Street the plateau beyond the Denburn had been thought of as a place for an ideal and modern town, such as Edinburgh and other cities were building.

Charles Abercrombie published his proposals probably in 1803 and these **Further Improvements** to the city proposed beyond the Denburn (where Union Terrace now is) a great Crescent. A few houses were constructed to that pattern, with short terraces at the north and south ends and open to the valley and Belmont Street, and behind the crescent was to be a large square. Further west, he proposed another square on axis with the first: while regular streets flanked by terraces made up a Parallelogram between Union Street and the Skene Road to the north. Craig's original plan for Edinburgh was obviously the inspiration.

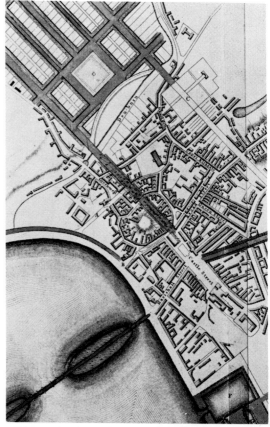

Right: Abercrombie's *New Town* with King Street and Union Street with the *Old Town*.
Below: James Young's unsuccessful proposal for Union Street and Bridge, 1801.

Brogden

76 **Golden Square**, 1810-21

By 1807, Abercrombie's **Further Improvements** had been somewhat reduced: his eastern square, with its four associated streets were built as **Golden Square**, **Silver Street** and **Lindsay Street**, between 1810 and 1821. Although of the same pattern, they are far from identical, and Golden Square does not form an architecturally unified composition.

The houses form the standard for this part of Aberdeen: two-storey, usually with a cornice, a low parapet partially hiding the slated roof. The arrangements of individual facades and the internal arrangements of rooms conforms to similar ones in Edinburgh, Bath or London: doorway to one side leading to stair hall with reception room of two windows on the ground floor (usually a dining room), and further reception room to the rear. Upstairs are usually three rooms, but it is unusual for the drawing room to occupy the full width as it does elsewhere in Britain. There were further rooms in the roof, and service rooms were on the ground floor, half a flight down from the pavement, and separated from it by a light airy paved court with iron railings. Golden Square became a centre for *men of business* from Edwardian times and many of the houses were refitted as offices then; some had stylish and confident remodelled entrances such as No. 1 and No. 7.

Apart from the rather stern Migvie House, c. 1815
77 style of John Smith, **Silver Street** houses are somewhat simpler and smaller with no paved area in front, most only two bays wide. At the north end is **Skene Terrace**, 1820, where a few tenements survive, two with entrance porch to common stair. The rest of Skene Terrace disappeared when Rosemount Viaduct took its place.

Huntly Street, from 1818-41

In 1818, John Smith proposed a second square,

Golden Square

Originally Golden Square contained a well, known as the Hammermen's Well in honour of the Hammermen, one of the Seven Incorporated Trades of Aberdeen. It is now to be seen in the entrance hall of the third Trinity Hall. Its place is now taken by the granite monolith statue of George, 5th Duke of Gordon (1770-1836), who raised the regiment the Gordon Highlanders. When it was first erected, in the Castlegate in 1844, the Edinburgh law lord Lord Cockburn was characteristically scathing — to him Gordon was *a base and despicable, but rather a popular fellow. A bad statue, but still very ornamental of a street. So far as I am aware, this is the first granite statue in Scotland.*

Above: Golden Square.
Below: Migvie House, North Silver Street.

Brogden

Huntly Place. In the event a street was laid out along the south-west side of a woodland behind Crimondmogate House (also by Smith; replaced by the YMCA in 1962). This street, Huntly Street, consisting of largely speculative tenements, further diminished the likelihood of a great formal scheme like the New Town in Edinburgh. But Smith's proposed square was 78 partly realised in 1841 when he built the **Blind Asylum**, an ample and handsome classical composition of five bay centre, finished with a wide *block pediment*, with lower wings at right angles. It stands well back on the north-east side of Huntly Street behind an iron screen and imparts much of the dignity of Smith's hoped for square.

79 **St Mary's Roman Catholic Cathedral**
Alexander Ellis, 1860
Exactly 300 years after Mass had been banned by the Scottish Parliament, St Mary's represented a welcome return to prominence by the Catholic community, of which its architecture is a celebration. Exceptionally tall, a handsome interior beneath the high roof of the nave, clerestory, plus aisles (with their own dormers), it stands skew to Huntly Street, so that the side of the nave and the Cathedral Halls, and the later spire add a certain movement to the composition and help break down its considerable mass. The spire, one of the tallest in the city, was built in 1877 by Ellis's partner Robert Wilson to celebrate the Church being elevated to a Cathedral.

80 **Dee Street** and **Gordon Street** from 1809
Dee Street makes an appealing enclave although threatened by unplanned commercial development; and the surviving houses, whether rubble, harled or ashlar, have charm, and in many cases fine decorative detail such as Nos. 52 and 69. At the south and on axis is Dee Place, a surviving pocket estate of three bays and two storeys whose placement gives it, and 81 Dee Street a dignity. **Jackson's Garage** (now SMT), Bon Accord Street by A. G. R. Mackenzie, 1937, is a rare example of excellent commercial architecture of the period in Aberdeen, while respecting its setting.

Bon Accord Square and Crescent from 1823
Archibald Simpson
Designed by Simpson for the Tailor's Incorporation (although Bon Accord Street had already been begun by Harry Leith in 1819), with a sense of design and 82 coherence for the whole area. **Bon Accord Square**, 1823 onwards (Simpson and Tailors parted acrimoniously in 1825), is curiously aligned parallel to the old Hardgate as if the new Union Street did not

Brogden

Brogden

exist. Simpson's special achievement becomes apparent
83 when a visitor turns into **Bon Accord Crescent**, a
long gently curving terrace of identical two-storey
houses overlooking the wide valley of Justice Glen. In
Simpson's original design the terrace turned to the
east to intercept Bon Accord Street, finally to run
straight to the Dee along what became **Springbank**
84 **Terrace**. Springbank Terrace was built much later
and is a mixture of tenements and houses in crisp
white granite, with an irregular skyline because a
group of three near the centre is only one storey.

Top: Bon Accord Square.
Above: Bon Accord Crescent.

Opposite, top to bottom:
Blind Asylum.
St Mary's.
Dee Street.
SMT, Bon Accord Street.

Brogden

Brogden

85 **Crown Street**

Crown Street, begun early 1820s, is made up of short sections of usually two-storey terrace houses. Beginning in the 1890s there was a burst of architectural activity at the north end, which continued past the Great War into the 1920s, the main building being the **General Post Office** (the fifth) of 1907 by W. T. Oldrieve (J. Cumming Wyness, designer). A turretted gable faces north up Crown Street towards Union Street; the building *steps* along the street into two further baronial sections before the main entrance is reached. As a piece of civic design Oldrieve's building is very effective: it calls attention to itself as a public building should, its form leading the eye into the curve of the street and beyond. Its craggy baronial form contrasts well with the severely plain houses of Crown Street while at the same time managing to suggest patriotic antiquity. An addition of 1964 (Ministry of Public Buildings and Works) carried on the townscape and strengths of the Post Office. Its basically plain facade is enlivened by its swelling curved shape and the sawtoothed edged roof which picks up the form and rhythm of the corbie steps on the Post Office roof.

10-16 Crown Street (including 1-3 Langstane Place) George Coutts, 1899-1901

All manner of architectural fireworks, designed by a much too little appreciated Aberdeen architect. Officially classified as Free style (which also means they are practically indescribable in words) their

Top: Crown Street.
Above: General Post Office.

intricacy will please anyone who cares to look up, specially since one has been recently washed down to its native whiteness. Diagonally opposite at the corner of Union Street is Ellis and Wilson's more restrained **Bank of Scotland**, 1892, although its bays and pedimented chimney feature and balustrade and urns at roof level echo Coutts' insouciance.

Prudential Building, 23-25 Crown Street
Paul Waterhouse, 1910
The perfection of Edwardian bounce in classical dress. Set in a curve of the street, its terminal bays face outwards from each other, the middle section divided into three parts which step up, and then down, one floor at a time. Add to that pilasters, venetian window, oval window, urns and channelled masonry.

86 **Britannic House**, 27-29 Crown Street
A. Marshall Mackenzie and Son, 1932
A plain seven bay front of three storeys with balustrade masking attic storey. Recently restored by Lyon and MacPherson.
  85 Crown Street is Jenkins and Marr's (Harbourne Maclennan's rather forbidding design) **Masonic**
87 **Temple** building, 1910, but it is exuberant too, especially in the broken pedimented central section and the gable and to the south (in Academy Street) with its absurdly overdressed round windows at ground level, and the bracketed block and sundial on the chimney stack.

Brogden

Brogden

Duncan

Top: 10-16 Crown Street.
Above: Prudential Building.
Left: Masonic Temple.

Top: Trinity Free.
Above: St John's Episcopal Church.
Below: Elliott's scheme for Rubislaw Estate.

Trinity Free (now disused)
A. Marshall Mackenzie, 1891
A fine, double pedimented, Palladian church. To the south is John Smith's 1830 former Greyfriars Free Church.

Baptist Church, Crown Terrace by James Souttar, 1870, is a rectangular building mixing Italian and 16th century Scottish styles. **St John's Episcopal**, 1849, by Thomas Mackenzie, is strangely *English* as Episcopalian Churches often were; its nearly island site reminds one of a Parish Church with Churchyard. There are late 19th century additions by Pirie and Clyne.

Skene of Rubislaw
The last phase of Aberdeen's neo-classical expansion was the private effort of James Skene of Rubislaw, whose estate lay on the open plain west of Union Place. Skene lived in Albyn Place, Edinburgh, and was impressed both by the New Town architecture and the prospect of the money to be made by a similar project in Aberdeen. Accordingly he had Archibald Elliot draw up a scheme for him in 1819. This was to be a mixture of linked houses and two terraces to the south, balanced by terraced streets and an enormous oval space to the north and finally a crescent looking to the ridge of Stocket *forest*. But as the lands of Rubislaw are more than a mile from Union Bridge, only parts of the southern section proceeded immediately, and the scheme was revised several times before completion.

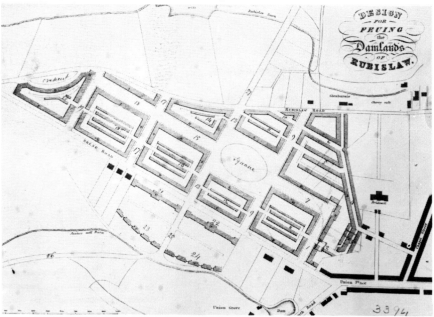

Brogden

Albyn Place from 1820

89 By 1821 several large houses had been built in Albyn Place, the handsomest being **9 Albyn Place**, now the Royal Northern and University Club, by Archibald Simpson; a symmetrical two-storey building with hipped roof, and a subtle movement in the facade — two bays with windows in semi-circular recesses flanking a semi-circular porch.

90 **25 Albyn Place**, 1830, is a two-storey villa with advanced end bays like pedimented pavilions which were added by Russell Mackenzie in 1865. Next door is a one-storey three bay villa (looking for all the world like a bungalow), raised on a basement, with rooms in the roof (the dormer window is later).

Brogden

91 **Conservative Club**, 28 Albyn Place
Archibald Simpson, 1838
One-storey but broad, almost rambling. An impressive neo-classical entrance hall. The only terraced part of

92 the original scheme to be realised was **2-16** Albyn Place, by Archibald Simpson who, in 1835, revised the whole scheme. He then sited Mrs Elmslie's

93 Institution, later the **High School for Girls** (1837-39) well back from the road, so that it defined with the earlier blocks of either side (both of 1830) a centre for the south side of the development.

Brogden

Top: High School for Girls.
Middle: Royal Northern Club.
Above: Conservative Club.

94 **Victoria Street** from 1843
Victoria Street introduces a curiously Aberdeen type of street, two-storey terrace houses on one side, one-storey cottages (with large dormer windows in the roof) on the other. The terrace block (on the east side) is made up of two bay houses with doorway tucked in. The construction is granite rubble and this texture is pleasingly contrasted by the sharp granite surrounds

Archibald Elliot (1760-1823) was one of the leading architects of Edinburgh in the period when the New Towns were created, and was responsible for building Waterloo Place and the Regent Bridge which opened up the Calton Hill to Princes Street; he also laid out Rutland Square and associated streets in the West End in 1819.

Above: Victoria Street.
Below right: St Mary's Episcopal Church.

to windows and doors. Glazing bars are a mixture of standard Georgian pattern, and the shortlived horizontal type (see 59 Victoria Street). The cottage row is made of two bay houses, and although these look small they are surprisingly roomy. The dormer windows have canted ends (like oriel windows) and are locally known as piended dormers.

95 **Albert Terrace** begun in 1839, probably to Simpson's design, was not finished until 1867. There are also classic cottages — those at the east with a half-basement and area.

96 **St Mary's Episcopal Church,** junction of Albert Terrace and Carden Place, 1862

Opposite, top: Melville Carden Church.
Below left: Rubislaw Terrace.
Below right: Albyn Terrace.

Of the Rev. Mr Lee, John Morgan recalled: *When I was sent on any errand to him, which was frequent, he generally appeared, not at the door, like any ordinary mortal, but at one of the windows, from which he preached evasion, and illustrated the uses of procrastination to such as could not pay. Poor man, like many another, he had begun to build, without first counting the cost, and as the result showed, soon came to grief. When the work was about finished, and a good amount owing to all the Contractors as well as the Architect, our Rev. Employer became bankrupt, and took French leave.*

Long known as the *Tartan Kirkie*, from its white and pink granites, and patterned tile roof. Its designer is given as Alexander Ellis under the close supervision of the incumbent F. G. Lee, although Russell Mackenzie is also credited. The *Building Chronicle* allowed it *some good points which make us look with leniency on the first thoughts of an amateur architect*. The chancel was bombed during World War II and the present is a much simplified rebuilding. The church went bankrupt during construction.

97 Albert Street, 1849
Possibly designed by Simpson, but built by Mackenzie and Matthews. Dressed ashlar is used instead of rubble, and the cottage side has a parapet, half basement, and often an extra bay. The highly ornamental Church standing, apparently, at the end of Albert Street, is the **Melville Carden Church** (originally Carden Place United Free) of 1880, designed by Robert Wilson, an elder of the Church.

98 Rubislaw Terrace (the west end is known as Queen's Terrace)
Mackenzie and Matthews, 1852
Rubislaw Terrace, which finally completes Skene's project, also introduces the next phase of Aberdeen's development and architectural taste, the classical anonymity and stern plainness replaced by Scottish (in the Sir Walter Scott-ish sense too!) It is a proper terrace: the carriageway and walkways are raised several feet above a communal garden (shared by Simpson's group of villas on the south side). Gables are much in evidence: half the houses has one, steep,, and crow-stepped, suggesting a 17th (or even 16th) century Scottish past.

99 Albyn Terrace
Perhaps by J. Russell Mackenzie
Sixteenth century French in style, the terrace stands forward of Rubislaw/Queen's Terrace, so the ample round towers topped with witches' hat roofs on its east end show up to specially good advantage.

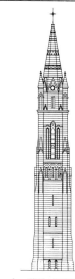

Neil Stewart

Alexander Ellis (1830-1917) was a pupil at Robert Gordon's Hospital and Aberdeen University before his apprenticeship to William Smith. Two early commissions for St Mary's Roman Catholic Church of 1860 and St Mary's Episcopal Church, Carden Place of 1862 established his skill in ecclesiastical work. He took **Robert Wilson** (1844-1931) as apprentice who, after a spell with Alexander Thomson in Glasgow, returned to Ellis in 1869. Ellis retired because of ill health in 1896. St Magnus Court, 22 Guild Street, the block to the west 1897, and the Station Hotel of 1901, illustrate the firm's later work.

Brogden

Brogden

Ferryhill

Ferryhill was Aberdeen's first suburb. In 1821 the open ground to the south was taken up with the lands of Ferryhill, partly garden, a few plantations, straggling groups of houses along the ancient Hardgate, and a few on its new replacement to the Dee Bridge, Holburn Street. There were mills, a brickworks, and the now lost Dee Village in the low ground. On the slopes of Ferryhill were several substantial villas.

100 **Willowbank**, 18th century
Directly opposite Bon Accord Crescent, this prominent villa was greatly transformed by John Smith in 1843 into a rather Italianate villa with *movement* — two gabled bays set forward, the east one more so, to either side of a classical porch (whose own centre section breaks forward).

101 **Rosebank**, late 17th or early 18th century
Now much altered and absorbed within a short terrace named after it, Rosebank was the later home of John Smith, who died there.

102 **Ferryhill House**, late 18th century
A squarish two-storey Georgian block with high, hipped roof, whose main feature are two segmental curved bays of three windows each (the centre windows of the upper floor were, until recently, *blind*). The wooded policies of Ferryhill House were defined by two roads which met at a corner south-east of the house: these became Ferryhill Road and Fonthill Road and formed the *backbone* of the suburb of Ferryhill built from 1831 onwards.

Right: Ferryhill House.

Round O

One walk took us through Roy's Nursery in Ferryhill (now built over), in which there was a deep depression, with steep sides like an old quarry and called the Round O. . . . *On my inquiry I was told by my nurse that two men had been playing there at cards on Sunday, and that the earth had opened and swallowed them up, just as it had done Korah, Dathan, and Abiram. I remember peering down into the pit to see if perchance I might discern the bones of the two malefactors whose death had thus become a matter of history.*
MacKinnon, *Recollections*.

Marine Terrace, Aberdeen. Edi Swann 1984

Duncan

103 **Marine Terrace**

Archibald Simpson proposed a prestigious and smart
row of houses to be called Belvidere Terrace on the
east slope of Ferryhill, above the river, with fine views
of harbour and sea. Framed by two-storey end
pavilions, and two-storey centre, the houses in
between were to give the appearance of one-storey
cottages (a full bedroom floor hidden behind the
parapet, and a full service floor tucked underneath the
house, behind a broad paved area). Only two such
cottage houses were built by Simpson, in 1837. The
rest of the terrace, now Marine Terrace, was carried
on by J. Russell Mackenzie and Duncan MacMillan
(by 1880) and the terminal blocks, added as late as
1967, are enough to make even a myopic property
speculator blush with shame.

Brogden

104 **Marine Place** also by Simpson, is a complete row
of five houses sharing a large wooded Green with its
own sweeping drive. These are probably the original
of the cottage type already noticed in Victoria Street,
and retain the original glazing bars (in the horizontal
pattern), doorways, and dormer windows. The
textured rubble walls are contrasted with smooth
granite cill course and dressings to doors and
windows.

Brogden

105 **Ferryhill Place** (from 1831) probably by Simpson is
in line with Marine Place, but disconnected from it.
The western part is made up of *half cottages* (there is
one *whole cottage*) with, unusually, long gardens in
front, whereas the later eastern part are a mixture of
terrace houses and tenements.

Top: Marine Terrace, drawn by
Edi Swann.
Middle: Marine Place.
Above: Ferryhill Place.

63

Ferryhill South Church.

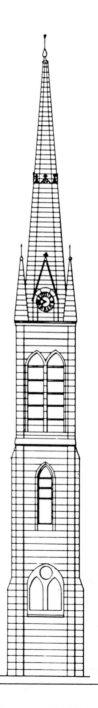

John Wilkie

Rotunda Place, 1-6 Polmuir Road, a terrace of four houses, is also probably by Simpson and is almost identical to Albert Street of the late 1840s.

106 **Abbotsford Place**, 1870s is a row of rubble walled cottages, and to the south (backing Ferryhill Place) is Woodbine Cottage, a small regular two-storey house.

107 **Caledonian Place** from 1859, James Matthews, is another terrace and row cottages scheme, in reddish rubble with some painted stone dressings. Bay windows mark the end and centre of the terrace; doors and windows above are also so closely spaced as to appear as doubles, and the stone ornamentation is coarse, band-like. The siting and nature of **Ferryhill Church**, 1877, by William Smith ought to be compared with the confident Free Kirk.

108 **Devanha House**, 1813, extended by Archibald Simpson, 1840. Taking its name from the supposed Roman camp at the mouth of the Denburn, it probably incorporates an 1813 brewer's house at the centre. Simpson was appointed in 1840 (perhaps as a result of a fire) and added the Doric porch and curved end pieces and rendered the exterior. Its extensive grounds were sub-divided in the late 19th century. The most imposing of the houses then built is **2**

109 **Devanha Gardens West**, by John Ross MacMillan, much influenced by Baillie-Scott with its white-washed roughcast walls, tiled roofs, prominent square bays rising into a parapet and complex composition.

110 **Rotunda Lodge**, Polmuir Road, 1864, is picturesque behind its high stone walls. Its interior boasts some extraordinary rococo revival plasterwork. It overlooks, and takes its name from, the Rotunda or Round O, a curious circular depression of obscure origin now incorporated into the garden of the Cowdray Club in Fonthill Road.

22 Polmuir Road, is a cottage version of Ferryhill House.

111 **Ferryhill (Free) Church** (now Ferryhill South)
Duncan McMillan, 1872
The nave of Ferryhill is large, ample and rather forbidding to the visitor, but, also in common with other Aberdeen churches, the tower and spire perform a genuine civic function, and suggest a spiritual one.

112 **Eastbank** (17 Fonthill Road) in the style of John Smith, is especially well preserved. This asymmetrical cross between *Elizabethan* and *Old Scotch* styles (in the terms of the times) with its angled gables and horizontally glazed (apparently) casement windows derives from Auchmacoy by William Burn (near Ellon) and Smith's Easter Skene House of 1832. This smaller version is the first of many of that type to be built in Aberdeen.

Duncan MacMillan (1840-1928) came to Aberdeen in 1861 from Inverness where he had been trained by Alexander Ross. He worked a few years with James Matthews before setting up on his own account in 1868, and within a few years secured the commission for Ferryhill Free Church. From 1878 to 1883 he practised with J. Russell Mackenzie when they realised Simpson's Marine Terrace. He was succeeded by his son J. Ross MacMillan (1867-1959) whose best work was his own house in Devanha Gardens.

Top to bottom:
Devanha House.
2 Devanha Gardens.
Rotunda Lodge.
22 Polmuir Road.
Eastbank.

Opposite, above: Matthews and Mackenzie's Design for Union Grove.
Right: Art Nouveau ventilator.
Below: Bon Accord Baths.

Brown

Right: Trinity Hall.
Below: 249 Holburn Street.
Middle: Holburn Bar.
Bottom: Granton Lodge.

Brogden

Brown

Brogden

Holburn Street

113 Some cottages of the late 1870's survive in Holburn Street, and one of the oldest Aberdeen tenements, **No. 249** Holburn Street is to be made into a Tenement Museum. It began its life as a c. 1820 house, becoming an Inn before being made into tenements. The **Holburn Bar**, 1965, by Michael Shewan is an exercise in modernism — white, flat roofed, the *structural* parts painted. The **Ferryhill Library**, 1901, by Arthur Clyne, looks like a cross between picturesque villa and granite gate-lodge.

Holburn Street northwards has a heterogeneous character. Simple two-storey buildings give way to taller blocks of tenements of the early 20th century with positive civic overtones at the junction with

114 Great Western Road. **Trinity Hall** (the third), 1964, by Mackie Ramsay and Taylor, incorporates tracery by John Smith in the principal upper section at the corner. The interiors are very dramatic.

115 **211-229** Great Western Road (originally Ashley Place) is a charming row of unspoiled 1870 cottages, set back with its own tree-lined carriageway.

116 Embedded in Great Western Place (8-14) is **Granton Lodge** (c. 1830, style of Simpson) a sandstone fronted villa with prominent half octagon central bay (entrance is at the side) and broad, overhanging hip roof.

117 The former **Union Grove Church**, 1888, by Ellis and Wilson is the earliest example of the re-use of a church as a block of flats (1978) and amongst the best. The corner block (28-38 Holburn Street) and row of tenements (4-14 Union Grove) is a civic contribution designed by Matthews and Mackenzie, 1887.

118 **Justice Mill Lane**
Note the curious gas main ventilator — art nouveau and cast iron. The **Odeon**, 1927, by T. Scott Sutherland (his first and only surviving cinema), is a curious composition of red terracotta and white granite. The **Bon Accord Baths** (City Architects Department, 1937, Alexander McRobbie designer) is one of the most characteristic 1930s buildings in the city, a giant buttressed granite box. Inside is much curved blond wood and shiny metal, the swimming pool hall roof supported on concrete arches. Note *art-deco* glazing.

Trinity Quay.

The harbour accounts for Aberdeen's prosperity and, despite its bustling and very up-to-date appearance, is the key to the city's history. Aberdeen was a seaport even before the Viking raider Eysteinn laid waste and burnt *Apardion* in the 10th century. For most of the mediaeval period it was confined to the quayside at the foot of Shiprow, but by the 16th century the Dee was creating great problems as well as great opportunities.

The deposit at the mouth of the harbour caused great difficulty at low tide, Jean de Beaugué noting in

Girdleness Lighthouse in 1840.

1548 that though the harbour was safe and easy, its narrow entrance more than outweighed those advantages. The bulwark on the south side at Torry was constructed early in the 17th century to cure that problem by increasing the scour of outgoing tides.

In the 18th century the Shiprow quayside was very greatly increased forming, incidentally, a pleasant terrace walk towards Futtie. The City invited John Smeaton, the famous Georgian engineer and builder of the Eddystone Light to consider further developments. He recommended increasing the north pier even further, which was executed in the early 19th century by Thomas Telford. Their work is best appreciated at **Pocra Quay**, and beyond. Also at Pocra Quay is the harbour master's station, the late 18th century *Round House*. The harbour entrance was later protected by the **Torry Battery** and less symbolically by Robert Stevenson's **Girdleness Lighthouse**, 1833.

Nineteenth century improvements pushed back the Dee southwards. The Upper and Victoria Docks, south of Trinity, Regent and Waterloo Quays were formed and, after the present course of the Dee was dug, the whole area was completed with the making of the Albert Dock and associated quays in 1870. Much land was reclaimed as part of these works, now occupied by the railway west of Market Street. After 1882, trawl fishing brought fish processing here, and the harbour has undergone further considerable change as fishing becomes less, and oil-related uses more, important.

Large boulders were often tumbled down from upper Deeside. On one occasion the harbour was blocked by an enormous one: Davie Do A'Thing (as David Anderson of Finzeauch was better known) had the bright idea of tying empty barrels to it at low tide, and, behold, it floated away with the rising tide.

Harbour and Dee Estuary in 1773.

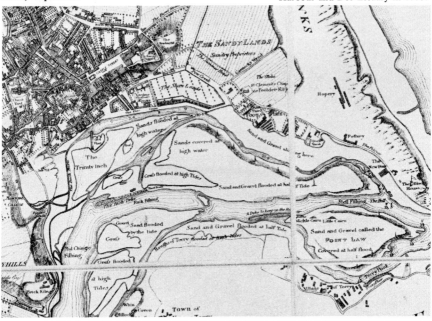

THE HARBOUR

The Mackenzies and James Matthews

The most prolific group of architects in Aberdeen were the Mackenzies; Thomas (1815-1854), Alexander Marshall (1848-1933) and Alexander George Robertson (1879-1963). They were the most successful, and even established a fashionable office in London.

Thomas Mackenzie (whose brothers also practised architecture in Perth and Dundee) worked for both John Smith and Archibald Simpson, before moving to Elgin to work for William Robertson (whose practice he took over in 1841).

Mackenzie's former assistant in Simpson's office was **James Matthews** (1820-1898) a grandson of the contractor for Union Bridge. He worked for several years in George Gilbert Scott's office in London, before returning to Aberdeen and partnership with Thomas Mackenzie from 1844 to 1854. Some of the work during the partnership is attributed either to the one, such as Thomas Mackenzie's St John's Crown Terrace, or to the other, such as Matthews' Rubislaw Terrace.

A. Marshall Mackenzie, trained appropriately by Matthews, worked for David Bryce (from whom he may have acquired his taste for success) before setting up in practice in Elgin in 1870. By 1877 he had entered partnership with his former master James Matthews. Work by the firm between 1877 and Matthew's retirement in 1893 is credited to both, although Matthews was very busy running the town's affairs as Provost between 1883 and 1886, specially concerned with the Rosemount-Schoolhill project. A. Marshall Mackenzie's masterpiece is the early 20th century front to Marischal College.

A. G. R. Mackenzie attended Aberdeen University, worked with his father and was attached to René Sargent's *atelier* in Paris, before he was put in charge of the London office in 1904. The Waldorf Hotel and Australia House were their joint works. A final burst of activity came in the late 1930s

RCAHMS

Shiprow

A visitor with a very short time in Aberdeen would see much of its history and future in a walk along the Quays. Beginning in the Castlegate by **Exchequer Row**, a cobbled serpentine way, first Shiprow then Shore Brae, leads down to the Harbour. Until the 1950s, it was still lined with tenements of varying age and distinction: these were swept away in the zeal for slum clearance and renewal to be replaced by a *complex* of supermarket, office buildings, parking garage and pub (1965-69 by Michael Blampied and Partners) not nearly as hateful as these buildings often are.

120 **Provost Ross' House**

George Johnsone, 1593
The only house to survive is the tall, narrow Provost Ross' House. The eastern section is the earlier, the five-bay western section, with its arcade is early 18th century. Some of the small rooms retain original features. Repaired by A. G. R. Mackenzie in 1954, and it now houses the Maritime Museum. The

exhibition within displays the story of the harbour's development — including whaling, trawling, oil and shipbuilding. *Open daily 10 am-5 pm.*

Further along Shiprow are remains of an early 14th century wall with doorway, pointed arch, slits, and other features, some moved here from elsewhere. These remains may be associated with the Friary of St Katherine (whose *hill*, now the Adelphi, is above and to the north).

At **Shore Brae**, the way turns south to the fascinating oil service boats, all bright, colourful and shiny. Unfortunately, Aberdeen's harbour is not exploited as a public asset as is, for example, Helsinki's which it closely resembles. Rather, the quay is rudely fenced off, with large warehouses hard against the road leaving pedestrians to share the cobbled Regent Quay with thundering harbour traffic. An appreciation of architecture here is perilous.

121 **Harbour Offices**
A. Marshall Mackenzie, 1883-85
A very curious building, flat like much of Mackenzie's work, the pilasters and pediment appearing almost as if painted on, the Harbour Offices are lopsided rather than asymmetrical. It looks as if the eastern end was curtailed through lack of funds, but that is the way the architect intended it: all comes right if viewed from the sea side.

A short row of late 18th and 19th century buildings leads to the end of Marischal Street, finished off castle fashion on the west side by two interlocking cylinders.

when the Northern Hotel, several churches, the Sports Pavilion at King's College, and Jackson's Garage (now SMT) were built.

At the end of the foremost neck of land there is a little village called Footie, and on the other headland another Torye, and both nigh in harbour's mouth, and lying very near unto the place where the ships usually ride, have given opportunity of much fraud, in landing goods privately, but prevented of late, by appointing the waiters by turns, to watch those two places narrowly. The trade of this place is inwards from Norway, eastland from Holland and France: and outwards, with the salmon and pladding, commodities caught and made hereabout in greater plenty than any other place over the nation whatsoever. Thomas Tucker, 1655.

Opposite: Provost Ross's House.
Below: Harbour Offices.

New Harbour Offices & Warehouses. Aberdeen.
Matthews & Mackenzie Architects.

Duncan

The **Clydesdale Bank**, 1902, by R. G. Wilson, faces both west, with seven pedimented bays marked by pilasters on a channelled base decorated with the coloured coats of arms representing Consular offices, and south, where Wilson tackled the *problem* of the narrow gable with a master's skill and turned it into the more imposing front.

Old Customs House
James Gordon of Cobairdy, 1771
An elegant, well proportioned, wealthy private house, conveying the impression — with its *Gibbs* door surround and quoins — of being earlier than its date.
Regent House, 1898, A. Marshall Mackenzie, seems two buildings. The first floor bows out, ship fashion and is carried on brackets. Step further back, traffic willing, to discover a second, classical building on top, slightly set back to make room for a pair of granite urns.

122 A row of late 18th century and early 19th century houses follows, of varied good detail — note the balustrade built into the first-floor windows of the **Stanley Hotel** (No. 39) and the Venetian windows with the (Loanhead) granite of **49-51 Regent Quay** houses give way to warehouses, some of which are ornamented with pilasters and rusticated basements, but they are mostly simple, robust, granite buildings with small windows. Some of these were restored by Thomson Taylor Craig and Donald as part of the Seaforth Maritime Group.

Top: Clydesdale Bank, west front.
Middle: Clydesdale Bank, Regent Quay front.
Above: Old Customs House, doorway.
Right: Old Customs House.

123   **At the end** of Regent Quay, the rail yards on the left are what is left of the old railway station for the North. Before the railway was laid along the Denburn in 1865 passengers had to trundle along Guild Street, Trinity Quay and Regent Quay to join another train at the beginning of Waterloo Quay. At the corner of Waterloo Quay and Wellington Street is a block of c. 1840 (probably designed by John Smith) of ashlar granite — segmental arches on ground floor, windows with architraves above.

St Clement

The quay ends here with the outer harbour beyond, and Hall Russell's Shipyard between Waterloo Quay and Footdee. A number of granite warehouse blocks survive in the area north of Waterloo Quay, but most of this area, indeed the whole of St Clement's Parish, has been flattened in the hope of attracting new industry. By far the most splendid survival is the

124 c. 1820 four-storey **Warehouse/Tenement** block that forms the south side of St Clement's Street between Wellington and Links Street which shows the sort of urban architecture John Smith had in mind for the whole district. The three-bay centre block is raised to form a block pediment, its full-sized central windows

Left: Regent Quay.
Top: 49 Regent Quay.
Middle: Seaforth Maritime, Regent Quay.
Above: Smith's Warehouse/Tenement Block.

Brogden

capped by a segmental arch. All other openings in the warehouse are squarish with segmental arches. The end blocks contain tenement flats above arched shops.

Note also the much smaller building, probably an **engine house** whose ends stand slightly forward and are pedimented: the large central opening is segmental headed. It is a lesson that ordinary buildings need not always be ordinary.

125 The centre of the until recently populous seafaring ward and parish of **St Clement's** is the 1828 kirk by John Smith and meant to stand on the north side of a large square. A simple large nave is given distinction by the three stage central, and now flat-topped tower. Many gravestones in the Churchyard of nautical interest.

126 Footdee

Brogden

At the extreme east end of the harbour, Futtie was laid out by John Smith as two squares of regular cottage houses at the beginning of the 19th century. In the 1880s the houses were sold to their tenants, and what has resulted over the last hundred years is a somewhat regularised disorder. Many of the houses have been raised at least one storey, some two or more, and the squares have been built on — with rows of *tarry* sheds. The result is a neighbourhood of great character — a cross between the neo-classical aspirations of Aberdeen, and the close knit fishing communities of the North-east.

The Links

The area between the North Sea and Aberdeen contains the Links, sacred to recreation — the **King's Links** to the north near Old Aberdeen, and the southern half, by Footdee, the **Queen's Links**. A kind of rough and ready golf has long been played there. The Queen's links has an amusement park, 127 **Codonna's,** which has recently acquired a centre-piece — a brightly coloured octagonal *shed* building filled with electronic games, designed by Thomson,

Brown

Craig and Donald in 1983. Its form pays homage to
128 the **Beach Ballroom** — the site of enchanted
evenings since 1926 when its design by Thomas
Roberts and Hume won an architectural competition.
Octagonal, high tiled roof with lantern, it boasts cream
coloured glazed terracotta walls — a real period piece.
There is an extension on the sea side (City Architect's
Department, early 1960s) itself now a period piece.

Trinity Quay

129 At Trinity Quay is the **Old Post Office** building (the
fourth) by Robert Matheson, 1875. Diagonally
opposite, **St Magnus House**, a new seven-storey
block (the last floor masquerading as roof — the so-
called *mansard* so loved by the Planning Authorities)
by Richard Siefert and Partners, stands out in
detailing and handling of bays from its contemporaries
to the south.

The **Trinity Chapel**, late 18th century, for a time
a fruit warehouse, latterly a showroom, is now empty.
The **Guild Hotel**, and two recently refurbished office
buildings to the west are 1897 by Ellis and Wilson.
The **Tivoli Theatre** (originally Her Majesty's) by C.
J. Phipps with James Matthews, 1872, is a rather
Venetian-Gothic looking building with coloured and
banded voussoir stones to the arches. The side and
back walls are concrete.

Masked by St Magnus House are the **Goods
Offices** of British Rail by William Smith (1865-67) all
that remains of the original Station. West of this is the
tatty forecourt to the **Joint Station** (J. A. Parker,
engineer, 1913-16) rather perversely built of
sandstone. There is a fine glazed roof, and the whole
building has been smartened recently. Behind it and
lending it a further measure of style is **St Machar's
House**, a modern slab block by Mackie Ramsay and
Taylor.

Duncan

Brown

Top: Old Post Office.
Above: St Machar's House.
Left: Joint Station.

Opposite, top to bottom:
St Clement's.
Harbour Master's Station.
Footdee.
Cadonna's.

The Guild Hotel, like the Street,
commemorates the benefactor of
the Seven Incorporated Trades Dr
William Guild. He was a son of a
rich armourer, but instead of
following his father's trade he
chose an academic life and became
in due course Principal of King's
College. In 1663 he gave the
Trinity Hall to the Incorporated
Trades.

Brown

Top: Station Hotel.
Middle: Trinity Centre.
Above: Douglas Hotel.

The Station Hotel
Ellis and Wilson, 1901
Tall ornamental gables and shallow bays symbolise comfort, cleanliness and good food.

Guild Street is terminated by the six-storey block that used to be Bell's Antiques (with bell-shaped pediments to the end bays) 1897, by Harper and Sutherland, as much of Aberdeen as many visiting ships' captains ever knew (for whom it opened specially on Sunday mornings). It was, after the Station Hotel, the next port of call for Prime Ministerial visitors before their sometimes awkward and difficult explanations at Balmoral. **Bridge Street**, 1865-67, which arches over the ancient entrance to the town, leads to Union Street. Note particularly **35-52**, Ellis and Wilson 1881, the specially fine Free Style block at the corner of Bath Street, Duncan Matthew 1880, and William Henderson's 1881 block opposite. The **Trinity Centre**, Covell Matthews Partnership 1979-85 — a shopping centre with parking garages — is entered by foot bridges from both streets, as well as through the former Trinity Hall.
19th century warehouse buildings and a few early 19th century terrace houses on arcaded ground floors survive between Guild Street and the Green. **4-6 Trinity Street** contains the remains of mediaeval building (perhaps William the Lion's Palace but more likely ancient harbour works) in the basement.

The **Imperial Hotel**, Stirling Street, 1881, by James Souttar and William Henderson is fairly good Italian Gothic. In Market Street is the old **Douglas Hotel**, more recently known as the Victoria, begun in 1848. It was extended by James Souttar in the late 19th century, but the two buildings were then utterly transformed in 1937 by A. Marshall Mackenzie and Son, as an exercise in Art Deco.

Market Street continues southward to Torry and forms the west side of the harbour. Abutting St Magnus House is the **Victoria Tower** by Thomson Taylor Craig and Donald.

Standing, apparently, in the midst of shipping is the pleasingly simple **Salvesen Tower**, a twelve-storey block by Mackie Ramsay and Taylor, given elegance by the splayed top floor (which contains the mechanical plant). **219 Market Street**, by Baxter Clark and Paul, 1970, designed as the headquarters of a food processing firm, is self consciously *sculptured*, and plays large areas of black, usually windows, against the brilliant white of the walls.

A group of decorated and idiosyncratic Edwardian blocks of *chambers* survived bomb damage in World War II: Jenkins and Marr's 162-166 Market Street of 1903 and Cameron and Watt's 168-174 Market Street of 1900 are worth repeated attention.

Brown

Brogden

Brogden

Torry (across the Dee and in a different county) retains its individuality like Old Aberdeen or Footdee. In the 15th century it enjoyed rights and some prosperity as a market. Until the Wellington Suspension Bridge was built in 1830, Torry and Aberdeen had no connection, and for years thereafter Torry was no more than the tiny village of Old Torry, and a collection of farms where Aberdonians often spent their summer holidays.

In 1868 the Dee was diverted to its present course, the Council proposing to build a bridge over the Dee and open up the area for development. These proposals foundered, but in 1876, after thirty-two people had been killed in a ferry-boat accident, the Bridge idea was taken up in earnest with the construction of the five-arched stone **Victoria Bridge,** Edward Blyth, 1881. Thus the way was open for a new suburb to develop.

132

Brogden

RCAHMS

Top left: Salvesen Tower.
Top: 219 Market Street.
Above: 168-174 Market Street, 162-166 Market Street.
Left: Victoria Bridge.

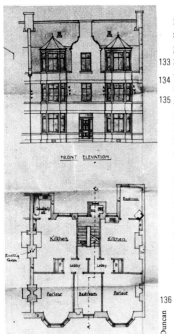

FRONT ELEVATION.

Above: Typical Torry tenement.
Right: Tullos School.

One of the new industries that arose, grew, and flourished in my time was Trawl Fishing, the pioneers of this enterprise in Aberdeen being Ex-Provost Mearns, now a member of the Fishery Board and Ex-Baillie Pyper of Hill-head of Pitfodels. The Finance Committee of the Town Council, at an early stage of the movement, appointed a sub-committee of their number to consider and report on the question of providing a Fish Market for the city and port. This Committee consisted of Treasurer Walker, Baillies Mearns and Pyper and myself. One of the first things we did was to journey south, and examine all the best existing markets. We went straight to London, and wrought from that homewards, commencing at Billingsgate and Shadwell, then proceeded along the east coast of England, visiting the following important fishing stations viz: Lowestoft, Yarmouth, Grimsby, Hull and Sunderland, finishing at Leith, and returning to Aberdeen by boat.
John Morgan, *Memoirs.*

Trawl fishing began in Aberdeen in 1882, attracting fishing families from Kincardineshire and other coastal settlements as far south as Northumberland. **Torry** grew with the trawl fishing and is almost entirely 133 made up of tenements which line the principal roads 134 — **Walker, Menzies** and **Sinclair** laid out on the north and west slopes of Tullos Hill by the City of 135 Aberdeen Land Association from 1882. Old Torry, represented at Ferry Road, Ferry Place and Sinclair Road by a surviving mid-19th century group to attest to Torry's pre-trawl fishing character, was replaced by the Shell Sea Base.

St Peter's Episcopal Church
H. O. Tarbolton, 1898
Very tall, its walls of pink granite setts in a concrete frame, its clerestory windows appear to rise from the roof level of the adjacent tenements. The suspended model of a fishing boat, a feature of the interior, has followed the fishing industry and been given to a Peterhead Parish; and the church is being converted into flats.

136 **The Garden City of Torry** was developed by the City with Dr William Kelly acting as Director of Housing after 1918 in a series of concentric streets centred on Tullos Circle. The houses are grouped in usually semi-detached pairs, and with their hipped roofs and harled walls, they resemble the comparable *Homes Fit for Heroes* then being built all over the country.

Tullos
In the 1930s, more houses were built on the southern slopes of Tullos Hill, and the modern semi-detached houses — their curving bay windows are expressed in horizontal strips — are good of the period.

137 **Tullos School**
J. A. O. Allan, 1939
One of the best '30s buildings in the city. A low block symmetrically arranged about the glazed semi-circular staircase (the symmetry somewhat undermined by the

78

Brown

Brown

east wing being half a floor lower to accommodate the slope of the site). Large steel framed windows (with characteristic horizontal panels) balanced with granite ashlar walls, the ground floor facing south is almost fully glazed, under a canted canopy to allow the classrooms to open onto a terrace.

South of the railway is the Industrial Estate, which has been expanded southwards to Nigg and Altens.
138 John Smith's fine perpendicular Gothic **Nigg Kirk** of 1828 is still prominent on the southern horizon, but
139 Shell's headquarters, **Shell (UK) Expo Ltd** by McKinnes, Gardner and Partners 1975-85, is more dominant; its splayed walls and horizontal bands of glass and concrete forming a landmark from many parts of the city
140 **Chevron Oil Company HQ**, 1980 by Jenkins and Marr is even more of a landmark. The architects chose forms which would humour its prominent position — the hipped slate roofs step up in stages, and the building is angled away from the city. Much drystane dyking.

Brogden

Top: Shell (UK) Expo Ltd.
Middle: Chevron Oil HQ.
Above: Nigg Kirk.

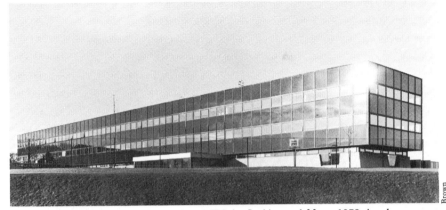

Brown

141 **Total HQ** by Jenkins and Marr, 1978, is a long, relatively low block, elegantly detailed in brown glass, a white wing to the south with splayed angular walls containing meeting rooms.

142 The **Altens Fire Station** (Grampian Regional Council Architect's Department, 1981) contrasts the glazed engine shed with its appropriately red fascia with the white, concrete block monopitch-roofed accommodation wing.

The other buildings on the Altens Estate are variations on sheds, and demonstrate what can be done using similar industrial techniques. **Press**

143 **Offshore Group** Offices, Press Architectural staff, 1978 contrast the dark lower floor with a cantilevered white upper floor — one largely glazed, the other largely solid.

144 **Sun Oil Offices** and warehouse by Covell Matthews, 1982, is a simple box-like shed relying on a composition of strip windows and contrasting tones of grey cladding for its articulation. Bruce and Patience's silver grey and red **Scottish Offshore Training Association**, 1985, exploits the variation in form and roof level inherent in industrialised building systems.

Brogden

Brown

Top: Total Oil HQ.
Middle: Altens Fire Station.
Above: Press Offshore.
Below: Sun Oil Offices.

Brown

Aberdeen City District

Until the 1890s, when it was incorporated into Aberdeen, Old Aberdeen was still a separate burgh, with a lively sense of its distinct identity and history.

The urban form of Old Aberdeen, or Aulton, is simple — a long, irregular street closely built up to either side, gardens and open ground behind. Its social structure was obviously weighted towards divines and academics; there was also a goodly number of county families who chose to spend their winters here. Now an inner suburb, most of the Aulton has been absorbed by the vastly expanded University of Aberdeen, which has rather heightened than diminished its charm and air of remote, truly collegiate quietness.

One enters from the south, at **Mounthooly** (apparently an ancient corruption of Holy Mount), bordered to west and south by high flats: **Greig** and **Hutcheon Courts** to the west and **Seamount** and **Porthill Courts** at the top of the Gallowgate (City Architects Department, 1966 and 1978). To the east is **John Knox Church** (from 1833, mostly G. H. Jolly, c. 1900), and to the north is **Causewayend School**, William Smith, 1875, a relatively ordinary Board school given a distinction it perhaps did not deserve by William Kelly's 1892 baronial keep at the north end.

Just across the railway, and alluding to its original function as the Aberdeenshire Canal is the early 19th century **Canal Street** and **Jute Street**. **King's**

Above: Alexander Nasmyth's painting of Old Aberdeen.
Below: Greig and Hutcheon Courts.
Bottom: Causewayend School.

Brogden

Brogden

F

Brogden Collection: Albert Duncan

Brogden

Livesley

Crescent, which makes a serpentine curve with semi-detached villas on the left and playing fields to the east on the site of the ancient sickhouse, or Spital, is contemporary. All the land northwards of here to College Bounds was owned by the Church and Hospital of St Peter, both already in ruins by the 17th century, and now surviving only in place names.

146 **Convent of St Margaret of Scotland**
Sir Ninian Comper, 1891
Only the chapel and one bay of the scheme to rebuild an episcopal nunnery was completed. The canted and buttressed chancel end of the tiny chapel seems to spring from the rock, and its high windows, and the trees, enhance its remote sequestered nature. Its high, narrow interior is magical. Under restoration by Lyon and MacPherson.

147 **Militia Barracks** (now the Corporation Bus Depot),
William Ramage, 1861-63
Simpson's not very prolific pupil chose an appropriately baronial form with crow stepped gables and turrets.

148 **St Peter's Cemetery** (entrance in King Street) is on the site of the old Church (remains incorporated in Moir of Scotstoun enclosure). It was begun in the 1830s, as a subscription garden-cemetery to the design of an unknown architect. The Hellenistic lodges (rubble built, with shallow temple fronts and splayed window frames) and the cast iron trellis pattern gates are specially interesting.

Top: Old Aberdeen in 1773.
Above, right: St Margaret of Scotland.
Above: Militia Barracks.

149 **45 and 49 Spital** are 18th century altered at the beginning of the 19th century and recently restored. 49 Spital is set well back (with entrance way between later symmetrically placed shops and gateway) and has two attic floors in the gable front, with two roundel windows low in the corners.

150 ## College Bounds

As the Spital descends towards the north it becomes College Bounds, lined on both sides by 18th and 19th century houses, usually of rubble walls (although ashlar is not unknown) with either slated roofs or red pantiles. Generally, the roofs have not been spoiled by large dormer extensions, and great care has been taken to ensure that the details such as stone paving slabs, broad and low granite curb stones, and the cobbles paving the street are conserved. Add to this mature trees from a variety of gardens, and a long gentle and slightly crooked descent from the Spital, and you have the recipe for Old Aberdeen's charm.

Snow Kirk

At **29 College Bounds** is the blocked up gateway to the Snow Churchyard. *St Mary ad Nives*, as the Snow Kirk was properly called, was founded in Bishop Elphinstone's time as a parish church for the town then growing up around his new college, and existed as the parish church until it was incorporated into the parish church of St Machar's in the 1580s. The church stood until 1640, and the small churchyard is within its walls. In the 18th century, it became known as the Papists' Burying Ground.

The houses are venerable, standing generally in ancient ground: and save that their beauty and tranquility of that spot have led to the erection of a few pleasant modern villas, dotting it here and there, whoever treads the one echoing street of the Alton for the first time, feels that two centuries must have brought very little external change. R. W. Billings, 1846.

College Bounds.

Brogden

Right: Crombie Hall.

William Elphinstone (1431-1514)
was bishop of Aberdeen, and
founder with George Keith (q.v.) of
the University of Aberdeen. An
optimistic, energetic and efficient
renaissance churchman,
Elphinstone was educated at the
Universities of Glasgow, Orleans
and Paris and immediately began
his life of service to church and
state. He was ambassador to Louis
XI of France and was sent to
arrange a marriage between James
II and Princess Anne, Edward IV
of England's niece. But his
persuasive powers were best
employed in securing support from
James IV and the Borgia Pope
Alexander VI to found King's
College in Old Aberdeen. He also
founded St Mary ad Nives, carried
on the rebuilding of St Machar's,
and assembled much of the
material to build the Bridge of
Dee.

151 It is now entered from the north through **Johnston Hall of Residence**, 1963, the somewhat more adventurous of the pair by Robert Matthew, Johnson-Marshall and Partners. Corrugated metal cladding was — indeed is — pretty advanced for Aberdeen. Its older neighbour, **Crombie Hall**, quintessentially '50s *Scandinavian* stands in wooden grounds between two Georgian houses. The accommodation block is harled and has a pitched roof, and a basement. The dining hall stands forward and has a large glazed east wall under a long sloping roof; communal accommodation joins the two blocks.

Powis Lodge, 1802, enlarged by Alex Fraser in 1830. Two-storey with large polygonal bay, attached to an 18th century cottage fronting College Bounds. The fairy towers of the gate to Powis Lodge, also by Fraser in 1830, provide rather Saracenic echoes of the spires of King's College towers which disappeared in the restoration of the 1820s.

Powis Lodge.

152 King's College from 1500

Sufficiently well ordered and equipped recorded Jean de
Beaugué in 1548: the College forms a quadrangle, of
which the chapel is the only surviving of Bishop
William Elphinstone's original foundation. The west
principal frontage is by John Smith (who did much
else to repair the College in the 1820s), the south and
east ranges are by Robert Matheson, 1860-62,
somewhat obscuring two early towers — **Ivy** (to SE)
and **Cromwell**.

King's College Chapel, 1500

The Chapel is a long, stoutly buttressed, aisleless
building, the east end finished as a half octagon with
wide pointed windows filled with tracery. Similar
windows are found on both flanks and over the west
door.

The 16th century tall oak screen of really excellent
workmanship, which separates nave and choir
comprises the finest mediaeval woodwork surviving in
Scotland. It contained confessional cubicles with
carved grilles (the confessor stood in the nave), and a
staircase led originally to the library. The blocked-up
door high in the south wall of the choir indicates the
original position of the screen. The excellence of the
screen embraces the choir stalls. The ceiling is a
shallow wooden vault criss-crossed by mouldings, and
the tracery on the inside windows, apparently

James Cassie's view of King's
College from the south-east
showing Cromwell and Ivy Towers
in original state.

Hector Boethius, (or properly
Boece, pronounced Boyce)
Elphinstone's lieutenant in
establishing King's College, was
born about 1465 and died in 1536.
Boece was a classical scholar born
in Dundee and later educated in
Paris where he taught liberal arts
and became a friend of Erasmus.
He was first Principal of King's
College, and wrote histories of the
Bishops of Aberdeen, and of
Scotland, and thus established the
status of both King's College and
St Machar's. His **History** earned
criticism. Dr Johnson wrote *His
history is written with elegance and
vigour, but his fabulousness and
credulity are justly blamed. His
fabulousness, if he was the author of
the fictions, is a fault for which no
apology can be made; but his
credulity may be excused in an age
when all men were credulous.*

Aberdeen University

Duncan

Top: F. W. Lockhart's painting of King's Chapel Screen.

The great glory of King's College is the woodwork of its Chapel. The carving throughout is of the most gorgeous and delicate kind, and it is as clean and sharp as though it were fresh from the knife. The diversities of the traceries panels are infinite in variety . . . there is no woodwork in Scotland capable of a moment's comparison with the stalls of King's College, nor will many English specimens rival them. R. W. Billings, 1846.

mutilated at the Reformation, present the rather coarse broad divisions now visible. We are lucky so much survives. The building was neglected to the extent that Pennant recorded it as being *very ruinous within* in 1769.

A squat tower of three stages joins the chapel, forming the north-west corner of the quadrangle. The bell stage has a simple pointed opening to each front (except the west which has two windows and clock face) flanked by stout buttresses. The glory of King's, and Old Aberdeen, is the stone crown on top. In 1633 it was blown down in a storm, and the rebuilding — assisted by a grant from the King — was commemorated by the King's initials in the lead fleche. The lantern also dates from this time. A two-storey wing on the east flank was built soon after containing a *Public School* on the ground floor and the great hall above. The wing terminated in the **Ivy Tower** (which then had a wooden spire) containing the kitchen, with small chambers above. Only the tower survived beyond 1860. The west wing, on the College Bounds side, contained rooms for staff and students, and at the end another tower, next to which were the Principal's rooms. Extra accommodation was soon needed, and a south wing finished the quadrangle.

The Reformation radically altered the College's character as an institution, and as a result the buildings fell into disrepair. By the early 17th century the chapel, then unused, had windows either built up, or broken. Yet in 1658, **Cromwell's Tower** was built at the north end of the east range to accommodate extra students providing six floors of four rooms each. Even more rooms were soon needed, and a wooden structure joined the tower to the east end of the chapel with a new stair tower. These survived until John Smith's rebuilding of the 1820s, when the interior of Cromwell's tower was remade into four floors.

The library was a small room built above the vestry, and both formed a sort of lean-to on the south wall of the chapel, until destroyed by fire in 1779. The books, happily, were pitched into the chapel and thus saved: for the next hundred years the nave served as library until the **New Library** by Robert Matheson replaced the 16th century hall and school in the east wing. It has only recently ceased to be the University Library.

The west side of the College facade was obscured by a lower grammar school standing between it and College Bounds which was removed in the late 18th century along with much of the west front itself. The stone was used to build **50-52 College Bounds** in 1780.

John Smith's collegiate *Gothic* **West Front** was built in 1832, replacing the south-west tower and the Principal's apartments with a museum and a Senatus meeting room.

The original south wing had been replaced by 1730, on the court side boasting a *piazza* (arcade). This was a favourite gathering place for the students, and was rebuilt in 1860 as classrooms, following the unification of the University of Aberdeen. At that time there was only one resident Professor and *no* resident students.

A new memorial to Bishop Elphinstone, commissioned in 1911 from Harry Wilson to stand in the chancel of the chapel, was so big, that it was decided to site the splendid bronze recumbent figure outside the west door — a blessing for both the chapel and College Bounds.

Above: King's College in the 17th century.
Left: John Smith's west range.

The attempt wrote Cockburn in 1842, *to maintain two Universities in such a place is absurd. They should have given up the one in the town (Marischal) and made the old venerable, well placed academic looking King's College the single seat of their science. It is vain to speak about a thing so reasonable to either of these two parties each of whom would rather see its favourite establishment in science besides extinguished rather than yield to the other.*

Brogden

Above: Elphinstone Hall.
Right, below: New King's.

New King's

A. Marshall Mackenzie, 1912

The northern arm of a larger quadrangle opposite the chapel contains lecture rooms of varying size, with prominent half octagonal glazed staircase bays with Gothic tracery and other details from the Chapel.

In 1927, A. Marshall Mackenzie and Son began the east *wing*, the **Elphinstone Hall**, set gable end to the new quadrangle, with two semi-octagonal bays along its long, northern facade. Elphinstone Hall, and its connecting wing to the original King's College, continues the familiar details — the *buttress* corners, crow steps, steep pitch of the gable end, and particularly the low and wide pointed arches of the arcade. The *unfinished* corner of this new quadrangle was completed by the **Taylor Building** in 1958 by G. Bennett Mitchell, an uncomfortable attempt to blend *traditional* and *modern* design.

Brogden

Brogden

Sports Pavilion
A. G. R. Mackenzie, 1939-41

One of the few frankly modern buildings in Aberdeen before the War which might have been recognised as such by the Continental visitor. Raised one-storey for views over the playing fields, and reached by characteristically thin concrete steps and balcony, Mackenzie's composition is classical, but in expression modernist. Each bay is a square frame containing five steel framed windows. The centre is raised slightly, its coving cornice extended outwards to form a portico.

Opposite (on King Street at Regent Walk) is A. G. R. Mackenzie's **St Mary's Church**, 1937-39: a composition of plain geometric shapes in multi-coloured coursed rubble comparable to Scandinavian work of the period. The tall nave has high clerestory, making aisles distinctly subsidiary. Church hall and offices carry the line of the aisles in a separate wing, characteristically for 1937, set at a skew angle to the nave.

The university buildings north of the playing fields and west of the High Street provide offices, classrooms and laboratories, with emphasis on flexibility. Typical of these are the Agricultural School (King Street and St Machar Drive, Mackie Ramsay and Taylor, 1972), the Zoology Department (Bedford Road, by Mackie Ramsay and Taylor, 1969), George Trew and Dunn's Central Refectory of 1971, and the Natural Philosophy Department by Thomson Taylor Craig and Donald whose domed pavilion provides visual relief from the slab blocks.

Above: Sports Pavilion.
Below: Agriculture School.
Bottom: Zoology Department.

Brogden

Brogden

153 **High Street**

From King's northwards, College Bounds becomes the High Street, although in this stretch the high chimney stacks are of berry red Seaton brickwork (the kilns being near Old Aberdeen on the Don). Interspersed with these are professors' houses, or town houses of landed families. **70 High Street**, c. 1820, in rubble and stone dressings is ennobled by a pair of curved bays, and a hipped roof.

81 High Street
Style of George Jaffray, 1780
The grander townhouse of the McLeans of Cott, back behind a handsome gate and wall (again Seaton brick) it has three wide bays, originally harled (now in last stages of decay) with quoins at corners. (Fashion informs the *science* of conservation as much as anything else. Picked stonework with stripped woodwork has been fashionable since the 1930s, despite much good evidence to the contrary.) The centre piece consists of a pediment *broken* by the unusually glazed first-floor window.

The High Street begins to widen slightly at this point, marking the commercial heart of the Aulton. The fragment of the old **Mercat Cross**, 16th century stands on a modern base in front of Archibald Simpson's former **St Mary's Free Church** (1845) now part of the geography department. **Wright's** and **Cooper's Place** late 18th century is a two-storey range; south of it, is **Grant's Place** an *island* row of one-storey 1720's pantiled cottages: all restored by Robert Hurd and Partners in 1965 on behalf of the MacRobert Trust, for the University. **104-106 High Street** (entered from courtyard) is a skilful adaptation by Oliver Humphries, 1982, for use by a disabled person.

Top: High Street.
Middle: 70 High Street.
Above: High Street, looking south.
Below: 81 High Street.
Right: Wright's and Cooper's Place with Grant's Place.

Brogden

Town House.

154 **The Town House**

George Jaffray, 1788

A quintessentially Georgian building (indeed its likeness has formed the badge of the Scottish Georgian Society for years) — in granite ashlar, it incorporates parts of an earlier 18th century building. Three-storeyed, cubic, the central bay with a pediment, surmounted by a square clock tower (finished by urns at the corners) it is completed by an octagonal bell house with high segmental dome and finial. Originally, the accommodation included *A Grammar and English school, and a Hall for the different societies.* *different societies.*

The street splits here becoming to the east, **Don Street**, curving and dipping slightly downwards on its way to the ancient Brig o' Balgownie, and to the west side of the Town House, the **Chanonry**. Originally, both the Chanonry and Don Street connected to the centre of Old Aberdeen without break. They are now separated by St Machar's Drive and its heavy cross-town traffic.

155 **Chanonry**

Cluny's Port, a small house west of the Town House (now *in* St Machar's Drive) was the gate house to Cluny's Garden, now the Cruickshank Botanical Garden (garden walls being a characteristic feature of the rest of the Chanonry). In pre-Reformation times

Chanonry.

Brogden

Top: 7 Chanonry.
Right: Mitchell Hospital.
Middle: 8 Chanonry.
Bottom: Tillydrone House and St Machar's churchyard.

the Chanonry was lined with the manses of the prebendary canons of St Machar. Now substantial, regular Georgian (no. 3 is George VI!) and generally early 19th century professors' houses form a gracious tree-lined approach to St Machar's.

Mitchell Hospital
(No. 9), 1801
An exceptional single-storey open court of alms houses restored and converted to cottages by A. H. L. Mackinnon in 1924 and 1965. **Tillydrone House** (no. 12), by John Smith, 1820, is a substantial two-storey (plus attic) house masquerading as a one-storey villa: three broad bays, a blocking cornice above centre, and long windows reaching to the floor flanking the doorway. The pocket *landscape* garden is contemporary.

156 St Machar's Cathedral

From 1370

St Machar's is a monument to Scotland's turbulent history, and its present state is universally admired for its venerable and picturesque aspect. Its *architectural* history is complicated and there are still unresolved questions.

The See of Mortlach was removed to *Aberdon* in 1130 perhaps to an existing church building: within thirty years a new cathedral dedicated to St Mary and St Machar had been built. Of this nothing survives.

By the 14th century the nave was *worn out with age* and rebuilding began about 1370 in red sandstone. A fragment of this work showing naturalistic carving of excellent quality can be seen at the east end of the present nave. It is thought that the foundation of the nave dates from this period although the actual nave was finished by Bishop Leighton in the period 1422 to 1440.

His work is in a very different style: it is granite, and stern, and more than a little military (specially the west towers which are identical to fortified tower houses) and its stout round piers, and arches, and small clerestory windows above might suggest earlier, even Norman, work. Leighton's nave was finished by the splendid very tall seven lights of the west window.

Bishop Elphinstone apparently built, or at least began, a central bell tower and spire. Assisted by Alexander Galloway this was a tall octagonal lead covered spire, like its contemporary at St Nicholas which survived until 1873, and both based on the spire at Perth. Elphinstone also began a new choir.

Between 1515 and 1531 his successor Gavin Dunbar built the stout octagonal west spires enriched by bands of ornamentation apparently in imitation of the central spire, and as replacements of Leighton's military cap houses.

He also commissioned from James Winter the timber nave ceiling ornamented by ranges of heraldic shields — the centre group representing the Church, with the Royal Houses of Europe and Peers of Scotland to either side — all in descending order of precedence. Dunbar may have completed the crossing tower, but by the 1660's it appeared with gables to east and west in the Danish fashion.

The Cathedral was barely finished before the Reformation loomed. In 1560 the Confession of Faith sanctioned by Parliament ended the Pope's authority in Scotland, and proscribed Mass.

St Machar's was (and is) the parish Church of Old Machar, as well as the seat of the Bishop of Aberdeen, and should therefore have been so nurtured, but the lead from the roof was removed in 1567 (it had already begun to *disappear*) to be shipped to

RCAHMS

St Machar's in the 17th century.

In 1560, the Barons of Mernes, accompanied with some of the townsmen of Aberdeen, having demolished the monasteries of the Black and Grey Friars, fell to rob the Cathedral, which they spoiled of all its costly ornaments and jewels, and demolished the Chancell: they stripped the lead, bells and other utensils intending to expose them to sale in Holland; but all this ill gotten wealth sunk, by the just judgement of God, not far from the Girdleness. The body of the Cathedral was preserved from other ruin by the Earl of Huntly, and in 1607 repaired and covered with slate at the charge of the Parish.

Although the churches were
stripped, it was done with more
care than is usually thought: *That
the organs, with all expedition be
removed out of the kirk, made profit
of to the use and support of the poor;
and that the priest's stalls and backs
of altars be removed out of the places
where they now remain, and situated
in the parts of the kirk where men
may be most easily sat to hear the
sermons, and such things that serve
not for that use to be otherwise
disposed or made money of.*
Aberdeen Ecclesiastical Records.

Right: St Machar's — Bishop
Leighton's nave.
Below: Gatehouses, St Machar's.

Opposite, above: Bishop
Dunbar's tomb.
Below: St Machar's, as drawn by
Alexander McGibbon, 1893.

Edinburgh. Repairs were ordered in 1583, but St
Machar's, especially the chancel continued to
deteriorate. Dr Guild demolished the Bishop's palace
in 1642 to repair King's College and he moved the
high altar there.

By the time of the Protectorate, the choir was truly
ruinous. *Old and weather beaten*, thought Richard
Franck in 1656, that *looks like the times, somewhat
irregular.* Cromwell's men removed the stone to fortify
Castlehill. But, however ruinous, the choir had
supported the central tower: which, shorn of its
support, collapsed in 1688, taking the transepts, and
the eastern end of the nave. The nave was repaired,
the eastern arch built up, and galleries which obscured

the arches (and what little light could get past them) were used. In the 19th century John Smith (who built the gatehouse in 1832), and later James Matthews began *restoring* the church. The ceiling was renewed. The plaster was removed from the walls in the late 1920s by A. Marshall Mackenzie, and his son installed the three light east window in 1947.

The old transepts and choir are kept now as a consolidated ruin, and Bishop Leighton's and Bishop Dunbar's superbly carved tombs are now outside, although the latter has an elegant light glass covering. The west towers have been restored by Professor James Dunbar-Nasmith as part of a general programme of repair.

North of St Machar's the ground falls away steeply to **Seaton Park**, and beyond it the River Don. To the north-east is Tillydrone and **Benholm's Lodging**, and to the east is **Dunbar Hall of Residence** (George Trew and Dunn, 1968) on the site of the Bishop's palace.

Across the Chanonry to the south is **Chanonry Lodge** (the Principal's House), Georgian with wings to front and back. **16 The Chanonry** (behind early 18th century garden walls) looks Edwardian but it is in fact, 1936 by A. G. R. Mackenzie.

157 Don Street

The character of the buildings is similar to that of the High Street. **20-22 Don Street**, 17th century, has an arched close leading to the back, and a circular staircase. **23 Don Street** is 18th century, and later restored by Dr William Kelly, 1938. Late 19th century tenements (**36** and **44 Don Street**, by William Ruxton, 1897) interrupt slightly; but **45 Don Street**, 1820, and the recently restored **Grandhome Dower House**, 55 Don Street, late 18th and mid 19th century are more typical. **78 Don Street** (Bishop's Gate house), dates from the 17th century, and **Chaplain's Court, 20** The Chanonry, incorporated fragments of even earlier work. Don Street becomes suburban at this point, and although it continues to the Cottoun and Brig o' Balgownie it is impossible to get through by car. The walk which passes the old estate of Seaton, whose walled gardens survive, is recommended.

Top: Chanonry Lodge.
Middle: Don Street.
Above: Chaplain's Court.
Top, right: 20-22 Don Street.

The area immediately north of the mediaeval core of Aberdeen was marshy. Until after the middle of the 18th century, it was known as the loch of New Aberdeen, even though the only water was a dammed pool behind Upperkirkgate. By the 1770s a new *street* called the Tannery ran northwards from Upperkirkgate to what was left of the *loch*. At the time of the more spectacular improvements of Union, Street, King Street and the Harbour, Tannery Street was extended southwards to form St Nicholas Street (thus joining Union Street to Upperkirkgate) and northwards, patriotically, as **George Street**. Until the comprehensive development fever hit Aberdeen curiously late in the 1960s (unfortunately as virulent here as elsewhere, stopping up Nicholas Street with an enclosed shopping centre), both George Street and St Nicholas Street were important shopping streets.

George Street

158 George Street has always been a homely, workaday street, today lined by late 19th century tenements with shops at ground floor, notably John Rust's former Bar at the Corner of Schoolhill and George Street, 1891. The shops still thrive, despite having been under threat for nearly twenty years for comprehensive development.

Loch Street is serpentine, following the line of the *loch*, with — at the north end — a few 18th century granite and brick cottages, in an advanced state of decay. **57 Loch Street** (the old Northern Cooperative Society Arcade), designed by William Henderson and Son, 1906 is a shamefully neglected glass *roofed* street, which connects to the **'Coopie' Offices** on the Gallowgate, a block of the 1860s, part dating from the 18th century.

On the Gallowgate the very fine, early 18th century **Gateway** with doric pilasters and good iron gates, led to **St Paul's Chapel**, founded in 1720 as an Episcopal Meeting House, replaced in 1865 by William Smith. Dr Johnson recorded a *numerous and splendid congregation* when he attended service at St Paul's and its importance to Episcopalism in Scotland would be hard to overestimate. The Church, still roofed, is sadly neglected.

159 **Northern Cooperative**
Covell Matthews, 1966-70
The building Aberdonians love to hate: alien to the rest of the city, but not without merit. A four-storey block, each storey cantilevered beyond the supporting columns far enough to form a characteristic and curious angular profile of ribbed concrete, with glass strips appearing to hold up the next layer. At the south end is the sharply angled entrance pavilion.

John Rust was born in 1845. He was apprenticed to J. Russell Mackenzie but was in independent practice by 1875. He resigned his seat on the Town Council to take up the post of City Architect in succession to William Smith in 1892. He also designed an extensive sea front resort. His Bathing Station has gone, the Bus Shelter is scheduled to go, but the Terrace with lavatories, life guard's station, etc., may survive. He also built the Kittybrewster Auction Mart.

Below: 1 George Street.
Middle: Gateway to St Peter's, 57 Gallowgate.
Bottom: Northern Cooperative.

Duncan

RCAHMS

G. MacCallum

Right: Central Bakery.

Brown and Watt

Alexander Brown (?-1925) was the Surveyor, and George Watt (1864-1931) the Architect of the partnership which began in 1891. Watt had worked in Glasgow for Campbell, Douglas and Sellars, and his Aberdeen work is a nice balance of the inventiveness generally associated with late 19th century Glasgow and the disciplined reserve granite requires. The Central Bakery, in 233 George Street of 1896 and 1897, is characteristic of their commercial work; while their tenements 1-27 Rosemount Viaduct are the smartest in the City.

Opposite, above: Technical College.
Middle: Old Trades School.
Bottom: Savings Bank.

233 George Street.

Duncan

Duncan

Central Bakery

George Street, Brown and Watt, 1897
Tall, late Victorian and confident headquarters of Hutchison's. The northern part of George Street consists mostly of two-and three-storey blocks in granite ashlar with modern shop fronts replacing the originals. The classical composition of Hearts of Oak House, **213 George Street** (five bays with three bay centre under pediment *supported* by extra wide pilaster), contrasts with its neighbour (205-211 George Street) a late 19th century tenement whose *dormers* have come together in an elaborate centre-piece of scrolls, chimney head, and balcony. **233 George Street**, Brown and Watt, 1897, presents high gables to two streets, the corner formed by a canted bay topped with a low dome and finial resting on a tiny *gazebo* which peeps out of the top of the tower. The gables have vertical strips culminating in mannerist chimney caps, or ball finials, picking up the rhythm of the main windows. Opposite, A. Marshall Mackenzie's North of Scotland Bank, 1883 (now Clydesdale), is pleasing. The John Street vista to the east is closed by **Aberdeen Technical College**, J. A. O. Allan, 1960,

an eight-storey block, on a two-floor recessed basement. The structural grid is *clearly and faithfully expressed* (in the terms of time) and the functions are suggested by differing treatment and materials. The varied skyline provided by a penthouse is typical of the firm's work.

A very early work of A. Marshall Mackenzie is the old **Church of Scotland Trades College**, nos. 261-67, its distinctive tower mostly Lombardic Gothic with buttress corners, but finished as short circular bell stage with conical roof, and chimney.

Brown

162 **Aberdeen Savings Bank** (now TSB)
393 George Street, Dr William Kelly, 1927
Entrance being at the side, the facade of this diminutive building has been composed like a toy classical bank in the Venetian manner. A smooth polished striped granite base supports a colonnade of doric pilasters and double columns which screen a rusticated wall. There is a Venetian window with lion keystone (obviously closely related to Kelly's leopards on the Union Bridge parapet) at the centre, capped by a full, academically correct, entablature with balustrade.

Contemporary with the opening up of George Street were **Charlotte Street, St Andrew Street, John Street, Craigie Street** and **Maberly Street**. Originally residential, much of the early building survives. **90-94 John Street**, a two-storey tenement has characteristic piended dormers — now in decay. **38 Charlotte Street** (a corner block with 90-94 John Street) and the south side of Craigie Street are fortunately reclaimed and spruce. The entire block between St Andrew, John, Charlotte and Blackfriars Streets is occupied by part of **Robert Gordon's Institute**, rather academic classical of 1920 by J. A. Ogg Allan.

Brogden

Destruction of a *Burking* Shop
Dr Andrew Moir had built a house in St Andrew Street in about 1830 and had instituted it in an Anatomical School. In the light of the recently infamous disclosures about Burke and Hare in Edinburgh and as bodies for dissection were difficult to obtain legitimately, the residents of Aberdeen viewed Dr Moir's house with some awe.

In December 1831, according to the Black Kalendar of Aberdeen, some boys who were playing in the immediate neighbourhood, observed a dog tearing some substance from the loose earth at the back of the building. They gave the alarm and, in a few minutes, some 20 or 30 people were on the spot; when two lads said to be tanners dug up some fragments of a human body.

Dr Moir's students took flight, and when the door to his house was forced open by the crowd so, too, did Dr Moir, and by a back window. Once inside the crowd

Brogden

discovered three further bodies; on orders from the Town House these were removed to Drum's Aisle in St Nicholas' Kirk.

By this time the affair was quite public, and it soon grew into a riot of thousands. The mob attacked the house, first by trying to burn it down, then by undermining the back wall, which collapsed, and then the front; to the cries *burn the house! Down with the Burking shop!*

Provost Hadden accompanied by magistrates and constables put in an ineffectual appearance. So too did the 79th Regiment, then quartered in the Castlehill Barracks but, as the building by this time was entirely destroyed, it was deemed more advisable that the soldiers should not be allowed to interfere with the infuriated mob. They were therefore marched into Gordon's Hospital by the Schoolhill Gate where they remained until the end of the disturbance.

In the subsequent trial of only three men, great leniency was shown because it appeared to have been the carelessness on the part of the medical gentlemen which led to this formidable riot.

Charlotte Street Free Church, 1843
A version of a Palladian Church, obviously indebted to Gibbs' West St Nicholas. Remodelled about 1900. **50 Charlotte Street,** early 19th century, has a good doorcase, off centre in rough ashlar wall, a crisp projecting cornice and short parapet. Maberley House, before 1810, is regular three bay, two-storey under hipped roof, enlivened by three bay Tuscan portico (rather spoiled by later dwarf wall). Handsome gate piers with original lampholders.

Rosemount
Spring Garden is an old roadway connecting the end of the Gallowgate (the northern edge of mediaeval Aberdeen) with the high ground of Gilcolms Land and the Stocket Forest, a narrow *finger* of higher ground running due east and west. Its eastern end became a suburb, Rosemount, in the 19th century and retains its distinct character. Throughout much of the 19th century, the southern slopes of Rosemount and the low ground called Gilcomston (between it and Woolmanhill) was industrial. The only survivor is the **Broadford Works** of the Richards Company which straddles the west end of Maberly Street. The north half presents a handsome granite warehouse to the street — sixteen bays and three storeys, arranged palazzo fashion: the four eastern bays are offices. The southern block, 1912, is a huge, imposing brick warehouse, articulated by pilaster strips, five small arches on the top floor of each bay, a central battlemented tower, and two smaller turrets in the northern corners. Note the metal catwalks which service the five large doors per floor on the north front.

Rosemount House, c. 1810
Behind 28 Rosemount Place, through the archway of a late 19th century tenement, is Rosemount House, one

Above: Broadford Works.
Below: Rosemount House.

of several widely spaced villas. Built of granite ashlar, with string and cill courses, and simplified *cornice*, it has a particularly fine doorway — large semi-circular fan light, side lights and columns. It was extended to form a short terrace fairly early on. Nearby on Rosemount Place are two 1870 pavilion-like buildings, one storey with broad overhanging roof of unusually shallow pitch, with cast iron columns separating the shop fronts.

Rosemount developed from the 1830s, taking in 164 Skene Square (begun in the third quarter of the 18th century), and much obliterated by the railway in 1865. **84-89 Skene Square**, early 19th century are noteworthy, especially the latter with its bow front and original shop windows. **Skene Square** and **Caroline Place**, linked houses and short terraces of the 1830s and **Rosemount Terrace**, linked cottages of the 1830s, form the edges of a triangular piece of ground enclosed by old roads. In the centre William Smith, son of John Smith, and best known as architect for Balmoral, built **Rosemount Church** in 1875. It is a composition of Gothic forms — nave, south transept and square tower (spire never built), lancet windows below, large round window in transept gable.

Top: Rosemount Kirk.
Above: Northern Cooperative Wholesale Warehouse.

One of the once numerous 19th century **Meal Mills** survives intact within the Northern Cooperative compound in Berryden Road. The **Wholesale** 165 **Warehouse**, Tawse and Allan, 1957, is an undervalued building of concrete vaulted roofs, and multi-coloured infill panels, somewhat undermined by the more pedestrian office block and stair tower.

166 **The Northern Hotel**, Kittybrewster
A. G. R. Mackenzie, 1937
When built, it was the smartest hotel in the north-east. Its curved south end, with broad horizontal strips of window and two-tone granite ashlar underscores the horizontality of the scheme. The continuous first-floor balcony indicates the location of the formerly celebrated ballroom. Despite unsympathetic treatment inside, it has worn very well, and could be restored to its glory.

Northern Hotel.

55 Westburn Road, c. 1820, is typical of the 167 substantial houses along Westburn Road, usually of pinned rubble construction with dressed stone elaboration.

168 **Westburn House**
Archibald Simpson, 1839
One storey to the south and west, with a shallow overhanging hipped roof, the long facade has a bowed centre of three long windows, flanked by two further windows to either side. The later veranda is exceptionally broad and ample, with thin wrought iron

Above: Westburn House.
Below: Elmhill House.

columns and brackets, with a low balustrade. At the centre is a pedimented *port cochere*. The west facade is pure Simpson: a handsome and severe classical Greek doric porch, flanked by single long windows. The north facade is a more romantic design, three-storeys in height, with a sunken basement and an upper floor tucked under a shallow gable. Westburn House is unusual in being built of brick with a stucco finish. It stands in the centre of even more extensive parkland, taken up by Medical Aberdeen. To the east, **Cornhill Hospital** for psychiatric disorders (note **Elmhill House** — eleven bays, pedimented centre, pavilion ends *and* two Italianate towers — and Asylum Lodge c. 1855 by William Ramage). To the west and north, is *Foresterhill* which contains both the Medical School and the Infirmary. The main parts are by Kelly and Nicoll of the 1930's. Distinguished additions in the 1960's and 70's by George Trew and Dunn, especially the block of wards to the west of 1972.

A series of streets run southwards from Westburn Road to Rosemount Place: **Mount Street**, linked c. 1840 cottages and short terraces, **Loanhead**

Terrace, 1870s terraced cottages with oversized piended dormers; and **Watson Street**, 1870s terraced houses and tenements. **Thomson Street** was built by John Morgan, whose 1879 house **Montarosa** (no. 57) overlooks Victoria Park. It is a cottage with a side entrance porch and a first-floor conservatory. *This was a pretty little house in a fine open airy situation*, wrote Morgan: *Our living room being for the first time on the ground level was a great comfort to my wife and the children.*

234 or **236 Rosemount Place** are characteristic of the cottages of western Rosemount, while further west, nos. **37** and **39 Beechgrove Terrace**, have more elaborate treatment, canted bay windows to sitting room, entablature on consoles over door, and two piended dormers. **248** and **250 Rosemount Place** are even more elaborate. The canted bay window is now a bow, with curved glass, a curving dormer above, the door ornamented with Tudor-style tabling carried on Gothic escutcheons, and the second dormer a semi-circular top.

Argyll Place and **Argyll Crescent**
J. B. Pirie and Arthur Clyne, 1880-85
Built by the enterprising contractor John Morgan in two-tone granite — white and pink — with further variation in the contrast of roughened and smooth surfaces, the canted bay windows are carried up vertically into a dormer above, making, in effect, a tower. (Some of these dormers — nos. 75 and 77 — sprout elaborate side pieces.) The dormer roofs are decorated with delicate iron sunflowers, and sunflowers appear also in a stylised form as *paterae* below the first floor cills. Stylised *capitals* on either side of the entrances and the brackets supporting the eaves (suggesting the tryglyphs of a Greek doric order) should be noted.

In the 1870s the southern slopes from Rosemount to the Denburn were still largely empty of buildings. Beechgrove Place and Terrace (as the old South Stocket Road west of Rosemount had been renamed), was built up as far as Fountainhall Road and engulfed the early 19th century **Mile End House,** and the later **Beechgrove House.** Beechgrove became the house of architect Tom Scott Sutherland who sold it to the BBC in the '30s. **Fountainhall** (now 130 Blenheim Place), an 18th century two-storey house with period gateway and ironwork, commemorates, through its original name of Fountain haugh, the days when reservoirs and cisterns dotted the area. The old 1706 cistern from Fountainhall is now in Duthie Park. James Henderson's **Westfield Terrace**, 1874, is a charming Gothic terrace with elaborate bargeboards, gables and turrets.

Top to bottom:
Loanhead Terrace.
57 Thomson Street.
248-250 Rosemount Place.
Argyll Crescent.

The Grammar School was considered *a large and important job, more particularly at a time when such works were few and far between. During all the time I have been connected with the building trade, I do not remember a set of steadier, or better working tradesmen, than were employed on this building. The builders in particular were a picturesque set of, for the most part, elderly men, several of them wore tall hats and swallow tail coats, with bright metal buttons, clean white trousers, and long aprons; some had been in business on their own account but had failed, and were content to end, as they had begun, by earning their daily bread by the toil of their hands, and the sweat of their brows. The hewers were a younger and more lively, if also a more commonplace, set, and at meal hours there was often a considerable amount of fun and frolic, sometimes bordering on riot and desecration.* John Morgan, Memoirs.

Grammar School.

179 Grammar School

James Matthews, 1861-63

Sited on the edge of the Denburn, the school marks the change in taste and ideals from the neo-classical purity of Simpson and Smith to the romance of Scotland's past by its use of baronial. Matthews had also prepared both an Italianate design, and a severely classical scheme, but in 1860 Balmoral and baronial style was preferred.

The Town Council of Aberdeen awarded the first premium of £100 to the best plan for the Grammar School to the designs of Mr George Smith, Edinburgh: and the second premium of £50 to Mr Matthews of Aberdeen. An anonymous correspondent to the local newspaper disagreed with the result. The design by Messrs Hay was generally admired — as alike original, beautiful, commodiously arranged and adapted to granite. In contrast with that design, what has the Council for their £150? Only two sets of mediocre drawings which a city architect could have produced at a tithe of that money. From altered circumstances, it is not in view now to proceed with the new building. There was a great decision, by a large majority, that, notwithstanding the plan had exceeded the limit of the expense fixed, the Town Council were bound in honour to award the premium. **Building Chronicle,** June 1857.

Brogden

80 Melville Church
Brown and Watt, 1900
Recently converted into flats, its tall corner tower with
open bell stage is capped by a tall granite pyramid
that Vanburgh would have been proud of. Diagonally
opposite is Matthews and Mackenzie's soberly classic
Skene Street Congregational Church, 1886.

   Mackie Place contains two buildings c. 1815 as
does the contiguous but formally unrelated **Skene
81 Place**. The group of four houses is composed as a
terrace with a blocking course over the centre pair, a
panel bearing the name, and an interesting segmental
fan light at the centre shared by two entrances.
Recently well restored by the City Architects
Department.

Brogden

Top: Skene Place.
Above: Mackie Place.

Gilcomston
The suburb of Gilcomston stretched to the east as far
as Woolmanhill and straddled the Denburn. The
ground here had been feued out by the City in the
18th century, and houses were soon built for weavers:
living rooms above were reached by forestairs (as was
common in 17th and 18th century Aberdeen) with
very low rooms for weaving below. **Gilcomston
82 Church** (originally a chapel of ease) from 1771 by
William Smith remains curiously detached from the
City. His son John Smith added the vestry in 1845: in
the 1830's he had planned a splendid new church to
have been built in Union Place, and similar to his
North Church. Unfortunately it was never begun.

   At the end of the 18th century there were 2,000
inhabitants in Gilcomston, increasing greatly in the

*In 1856 Gilcomston and its
surroundings were pretty much in the
open country, indeed as was to a
large extent the tract of land
extending from Skene Square to the
Short Loanings, now for the most
part covered by busy streets, public
works and crowded tenements.
Carden Howe, a deep ravine through
which the Denburn flowed, divided
the school site from the city on the
south side, while the Gilcomston
Burn flowed openly. Morgan's
Memoirs.*

H

The Aberdeen Tenement is a distinct type, and while its architectural form admits of considerable variation, all tenements are basically similar: granite built, a staircase most often wooden, at the centre of the block to the rear, reached by a passage from the central front door. There are usually two or three more floors, plus an attic whose mansard roof makes it practically identical to the one below, with two flats on each floor: one larger with two rooms to the front and a kitchen to the rear; its neighbour simply one room and kitchen.

The kitchen was the living room, a sink in the window, a range in the fireplace and a bed recess. The character of these rooms varies greatly — from neat rather lady-like sitting rooms to busy, untidy and crowded work rooms. The common stairs are looked after on a rota basis (naturally the occasion of lively disputes from time to time). In some grander tenements, there may be a common loft space for storage or clothes drying: more usually, a *green* at the back of the blocks, facing which are the wash-house, commonly with boilers, a *cellar* for each flat, and usually a lavatory per flat. Otherwise — even in better grade tenements, lavatories would be on the landing.

Why there should have been such poor provision of plumbing is a mystery. It remained a characteristic feature of Aberdeen tenements until the 1970s, when central government funding became available to bring such properties up to standard.

The few tenements built by the local authority in the 19th century, east of King Street at the Junction of Urquhart Road and Park Road, were minimum standard even then, consisting of one room flats and two room flats in about equal numbers. The vast majority were built privately for rent, although most now are occupied by their owners. An interesting modern *tenement* tail-piece has been added to Seaforth Road, by David Brown Architects, 1982.

19th century. It was connected to Aberdeen by the steep and crooked Mutton Brae at the west end of Schoolhill below the Triple Kirks and merged with the city at the end of Union Terrace.

By 1880 the population of the city had increased from under 30,000 to over 100,000 and while some of this extra population was housed in new areas, much of it crowded into the older parts of the city, especially Shiprow, Broad Street, the Gallowgate and Gilcomston. In the 1880s, a solution was resolved upon beginning a new burst of civic and architectural activity, comparable to the building of Union Street.

Rosemount and Denburn Viaduct
William Boulton, 1886

It being decided to join South Mount Street in Rosemount to Schoolhill, at the Schoolhill end, the Denburn Viaduct was constructed over the railway, Denburn Road and Mutton Brae being obscured from Union Bridge and gardens. By judicious embankment, Union Terrace was given a more satisfactory termination, thus creating the site for the Theatre,

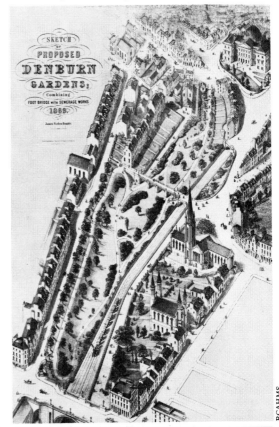

Brogden

Opposite: Union Terrace and Denburn before the improvements of 1886.

Top left: Mount Street.
Left: Esslemont Avenue.
Below: Richmond Street and Rosemount Place.
Bottom: 92 Rosemount Place.

Duncan

new church and Library. Cliffs of buildings to either side of the Rosemount viaduct approach were provided: but instead of terraced houses as in Marischal Street and Union Street, they were tenements.

Rosemount

Rosemount is an excellent place to observe the Aberdeen tenement. In **West Mount Street** and **Richmond Street** are some of the earliest from the 1870s, in narrow streets with an old world feel. Many use a wall-head gable in a very rudimentary form as the location for any architectural ornament. **Wallfield Place, Wallfield Crescent** and **Esslemont Avenue** have plain tenements with no front garden, whereas **Whitehall Place**, facing the Grammar School grounds, is rather grander, with decorated wall head gables and small front gardens as well.

As in **Rosemount Place**, ground floor flats can readily be made into shops, so that neighbourhood shopping centres can grow or contract without wholesale change to the district.

Right: 96-120 Rosemount Viaduct.
Below: Souttar's design for 96-120 Rosemount Viaduct.

Brogden

Duncan

185 **96-120 Rosemount Viaduct**
James Souttar, 1887
The first group of smart, larger, tenement blocks of rockfaced granite with smooth white granite ornament, most of the detail at parapet level — notably a pair of turrets with Gothic decoration above the grouped centre windows.

186 **46-80, 57-85** and **31-45 Rosemount Viaduct**
Alexander MacKay, 1887
Flanking the Viaduct approach (thus as much as four floors taller than is immediately apparent), these groups of five- and six-storey tenement blocks are of the standard type, the western range with three groups of paired windows, and paired chimneys with pediment between at wallhead. Pilaster strip ornament at the margins are paired to neighbours under tiny pediments. The eastern group has a single window at the centre and a triumphal arch-like treatment to the wallhead gable. The corner with Skene Street has a raised three-storey corner feature facing towards the Triple Kirks.

187 **1-27 Rosemount Viaduct**

Brown and Watt, 1897

The final group of tenements facing the Central Library, pretending to be a mansion block of flats (such as were currently becoming the vogue in London) are simply six blocks of Aberdeen tenements, with the wallhead features. The corner is topped by a tall conical roof with gazebo finial. This is by far the most *urban* of the tenement blocks, made so simply by dressing it in Sunday best.

A. H. L. Mackinnon's curving block connects Rosemount Viaduct to Union Terrace.

188 Two groups of three blocks in **Short Loanings** (City Architects Department 1935) restate the traditional tenement in almost modernistic terms. The roof appears flat (in fact it hides behind a parapet) and the sheer granite walls rely entirely on the arrangement of the windows for interest — the stair window at half level, and the grouping of the square windows into a horizontal band at ground floor level.

189 **Rosemount Square**, City Architects Department, 1938, completed by Leo Durnin, 1945-46. A wall of tenements curving round the edge of the site, the stair entrances on the inside facing the *square* (a greatly enhanced version of the back green). The exterior presents a public and dignified aspect, with good period detail in the horizontal steel windows of the flats, contrasting with vertical strips to the staircases. The great arch, overtly recalling the Karl Marx Hof in Vienna, has excellent low relief sculpture above it by T. B. Huxley-Jones.

Above: 1-27 Rosemount Viaduct.
Left: Rosemount Square.

Housing from a Woman's Point of View (1939)

The housewife's real problem is the expense of keeping up the four- or five-roomed house as compared with the one or at most two rooms in the crowded slums. This is a very serious problem for the woman whose income has not expanded like her dwelling. In addition to budget difficulties, there is her own and her family's re-adjustment to the new environment — not an easy matter for folk born and bred in the congested slums. Another trouble is the cost of transport to an from work, for the new housing schemes are mostly on the outskirts of the town. . . . The newer plans to have large blocks of flats in Central areas will therefore be very welcome. The blocks in Willowbank are practically completed and have been carefully planned, with many new improvements.

The new block planned for Morton's site (Rosemount Square) is likely to be even better still, and if only there could be more hired furnishings would be almost ideal, for this would save the weekly drain on the housewife's money of the instalments for furnishing.

An Onlooker *City of Aberdeen Housing and Town Planning* 1939.

In the later 19th century the character of urban development changed. The new streets appear wider, houses are more often detached and almost always seem ample, if not grand. In the broad vacant lands to the west there developed areas of substantial family houses, many expressing artistic aspirations in their owners, as well as gratifying the desire for the exhibition of wealth and fortune. Generally known as 190 the West End, this section begins at **Queen's Cross**, a *rondpoint* marked by a statue of old Queen Victoria, at the junction of Albyn Place and Carden Place: Queen's Road (as Skene or Alford Road is henceforth known) is the spine to this district.

Rubislaw Church
J. Russell Mackenzie, 1875

The Established Church in Aberdeen had been able to do little more than survive after its Ministers and congregation *walked out* in 1843, but by the 1870s it was strong enough to establish three new parishes in the new suburbs of Ferryhill, Rosemount and Queen's Cross. It was this Church at Queen's Cross which spurred the thrusting and energetic Frees to the challenge with Pirie's masterpiece. The Parish Church seems small, curiously and perversely built of sandstone and is distinguished by its later, rather collegiate gothic tower with prominent leaded spire.

Right: Rubislaw Church.

J. Russell Mackenzie
Trained by Simpson's successors Mackenzie and Matthews, Russell Mackenzie began practice in Aberdeen about 1860 after a spell in York. He and Duncan MacMillan were in partnership from 1878 to 1883 when Russell Mackenzie became bankrupt — as gossip had it, because his wife *flew too high*. Despite a public testimonial in 1888 he and his wife thought South Africa presented a brighter future than Aberdeen. He built the Goldfield Club in Johannesburg before his sudden death in 1889. His talents as an architect are best seen at Queen's Cross.

110

Brian McArthur

John Bridgeford Pirie (1852-1890) and **Arthur Clyne** (1852-1923) formed a brief but brilliant partnership before Pirie's death from tuberculosis. Pirie was a pupil of Alexander Ellis and draughtsman with James Matthews for ten years, but he learned much from his friend and third *partner*, the contractor John Morgan (1844-1906).

Pirie and Clyne designed Argyll Place and Crescent, and the curious Hamilton Place for Morgan. Pirie designed Morgan's own House, 50 Queens Road. Although not quite Pirie's equal in talent, Clyne was far from dull as for instance his St Devenick's Episcopal Church shows.

Queen's Cross Church.

Queen's Cross (Free) Church
J. B. Pirie, 1881

Built as a Free Church, the largest and most powerful challenge to the Established Church. Many of its most successful members were moving into the western areas, and naturally wanted a church close at hand, purchasing at considerable expense the last empty site in Skene's development: the prominent triangular space between Albyn and Carden Place. The Church was put out to competition, and won by young J. B. Pirie, a decidedly individual, skilful and surprising designer. Pirie's tall nave with its pointed west window of French detailing is enriched by his tower: the columns in the second and third stages are absurdly short, their capitals caricatures. The corner pinnacles of the first stage seem too large as, do the gablets around the spire of the second stage; yet the composition succeeds and could be no other way.

The **Convent of the Sacred Heart School** was created out of Westwood, 1864, built probably by J. Russell Mackenzie, for a very rich tea planter who never occupied it.

Brogden

Brogden

Duncan

An ingenious single-storey double villa at the corner of Fountainhall Road has a spiky richness, and complexity of porches, bays, decorated dormers, and wrought iron ridge decoration. In the same vein is **1 Queen's Cross**, 1865, also by J. Russell Mackenzie, a cross between castle and villa, with a rather French flavour: a two-storey L-plan house, with octagonal entrance tower, with shaped dormers, high roof with crown of wrought iron work, *and* smartly asymmetrical witches' hat tower.

Queen's Gardens
J. Russell Mackenzie, c. 1880
The last composed terrace in Aberdeen: terraced houses, three bays, two floors with double tier of dormers in proper Mansard (or, at least, French) roof with wrought iron continuous balcony at first floor level. The terrace is emphasised at centre and ends by houses by Ellis and Wilson, 1884, with prominent half octagonal bay windows, with a tripartite, almost Venetian, window and pediment above.

South of Queen's Cross, on lands generally feued out by the Incorporation of Seven Trades (particularly the Hammermen), is a greater variation in house type: tenements over shops, with adjacent family houses at 8-10 **St Swithin Street** (1886); straightforward [191] tenements in the leafy and distinctly superior **Union** [192] **Grove** (292-300 by George Milne of 1898 are typical); hybrids such as **72-78 Forest Avenue**, G. F. [193] Anderson, 1911, which has larger flats (with bathrooms!) and of course individual family houses such as George Coutts' **321 Great Western Road** of 1886.

Public buildings in this area include George Watt's **Holborn Free Church**, Great Western Road, and Brighton Place of 1894, and Jenkins and Marr's [194] **Ashley Road School** of 1887.

Top: Fountainhall Road and Queen's Cross.
Middle: Queen's Gardens.
Above: Forest Road tenements.

More characteristic of the West End are the northern streets, feued out by the City of Aberdeen Land Association (familiarly CALA). In **Devonshire Road** or **Gladstone, Beaconsfield, Carlton** and **Desswood Places**, only the materials distinguish them from their contemporaries elsewhere in Britain — typically two-storey buildings, with canted bay windows to the side capped by its own roof and often ornamented by wrought iron finial. The doorway is broad, often with an architrave window. Some architects varied this formula, to good effect. **4-6 Beaconsfield Place** (James Souttar) is a pair of houses where curved bays are positioned side by side, a gable above, simply but effectively articulated.

Fountainhall Road
George Coutts, 1884-86

Nos. **28-30** and **32-34** have canted bays, the same gables as Beaconsfield Place and grouped doors and bays together for rhythmic effect. In Nos. **36-42**, the emphasis is on the doorway, by the simple expedient of a gable, the canted bay ornamented by a pediment and carried up into the first floor as a tripartite window. Nos. **44 and 46** have bow windows with domic tops and the corner house has a tower at the corner for the door, raised up into a pointed dome.

Top: Desswood Place.
Middle: Typical West End house.
Above: 4-6 Beaconsfield Place.
Left: Fountainhall Road.

Above and below: Hamilton Place.

197 **Hamilton Place**
Pirie and Clyne, 1880s

For variety, imagination, and even wit, this series of large semi-detached houses for the builder John Morgan is unsurpassed. Each has two full storeys plus gable, the entrance to the side, and canted bays.

Near the middle of the group is a pair of blocks whose *Greek* details recall the Glasgow architect Alexander Thomson. These can stand as representative of Hamilton Place's richness. A rather shallow bay on the first floor, the corners marked by pillars with extraordinarily archaic capitals, is held in place by a stout pillar rising between the ground floor windows with a *cap* ornamented with decoration derived from the anthemion. The bay features rise into the gable by means of a stone roof whose centre supports a roundel with shell motif to its centre. The roundel also occupies the middle of a long, low, three part *window* in the gable in which the amount of space left over for glass is practically none. There is a pitched pediment above. The windows are ornamented by two capitals (recalling the one in the shaft under the bay), another acroterion and a couple of Pirie's favourite sunflower *paterae*. The doorway is set deep with the horseshoe curved frame with anethemion —

thus niftily managing to sum up the Greek revival and usher in *art nouveau*. An ornamental rain-waterhad with down pipe, held in place by pairs of sunflowers, separates one house from its neighbour.

At the northern corners of Hamilton Place and Fountainhall Road are two houses by Pirie and Clyne: the eastern house has a large turret growing from the south-west corner, whereas the western repeats the rhythm of the Fountainhall Road houses, the bay (and gable feature above) ornamented with *Greek* motifs. The gable to Hamilton Place has only three openings, in the centre. The doorway is distinguished by the addition of Pirie's *waves* and roundel above.

Kings Gate

198 **Kings Gate,** an extension to the west of Rosemount Place and Beechgrove Terrace is somewhat more pretentious. The houses are detached, although still closely spaced, and each exhibits individuality with more than a hint at the castle style. **Ernan Lodge** (82 Beechgrove Terrace), a decorated cottage, introduces a number of mini-castles; Nos. 19 and 20 are basic Aberdeen house types, with the additions of a square tower. **Kingsacre** (no. 16), has a tower, plus French peaked roof with dormers and crown. Mixed with these are pairs of large houses, Italianate small mansion houses, and somewhat baronial hybrids. **Atholl Hotel** (no. 54 Kings Gate), 1860, has the characteristic baronial form of turret, crow-stepped gable features, bow windows rising into *tower* with decorative dormers, combined with a wing of 1880 which looks for all the world like a dry-run for Marischal College. To the equilateral triangle gable, with roundel and horizontally linked windows, are added three sets of oval headed windows with gothic tracery: all held together by ornamental strips.

Top: Hamilton Place and Fountainhall Road.
Above: 16 Kings Gate.
Below: Kings Gate.

199 **Beechgrove Church**
Brown and Watt, 1896
Built as a Free Church, typically tall and confident in white granite with open bellstage, and spire. The
200 handsome classical **Mile End School** is by A. H. L. Mackinnon: note the equally handsome Servitor's House at the corner of the Schoolyard.

Below Kings Gate is an area dotted with little castles and chalets, the result of sober men of business leaving their plain houses in Bon Accord Square and elsewhere, to build a dream in Rubislaw Den. The junction of Forest Road and Rubislaw Den North is characteristic: 54 Kings Gate forms a splendid termination to the north, with James Matthews'
201 French, **Queens Gate,** 1871, to the south. On the west side, **1 Rubislaw Den North**, 1909, by George Coutts has a facade of warm pink granite in a richly varied mixture of bay windows, low eaved porch, oriel window, gables decorated with timber screens, prominent chimneys and half timbered extravagant billiard room at the top, under a red tiled roof.

28 Forest Road is a sterner, simpler house, with tower and conical roof to give it a castle air. No. 26 is cosmopolitan — (it would be quite happy in Bournemouth) — a pebble encrusted timbered gable, balanced by jaunty witch's hat roof over octagonal tower, a trim white balcony adding a nautical touch. Where Desswood and Beaconsfield Places join Forest Road is **Callan Lodge**, by A. Marshall Mackenzie, a similar house with a complexity of gables and roofs facing in several directions.

Top: Beechgrove Church.
Above: Callan Lodge.
Right: 1 Rubislaw Den North.

George Coutts
No personal details are known of Coutts, apart from the fact that he practised from the mid 1880s from premises in John Street. His two tall blocks of shops and chambers 10-16 Crown Street, and a trio of houses — 90, 92 and 94 Queens Road well illustrate his mature style. His early houses in Fountainhall Road are equally good.

202 5 Rubislaw Den North
William Ruxton, 1900
Built as one house it has been subsequently divided
into three large parts. The gables with their wooden
screens, and the bays and chimneys give it a ground-
hugging appearance, the two most notable features
from the street side being the billiard room bay (to the
east) and the enormous windows lighting the lounge-
hall, which takes up a large part of the north front.

Beyond the soberly Tudor **Kimberley** (no. 9), is
no. 15 **Glenburnie Lodge**, 1928, a late English Arts
and Crafts house by Clement George: rough cast
walls, low and large red tile roofs, and prominent
03 gables. The spooky **Rubislawden House** (also known
as Gordon House), 1881, architect (if any) thankfully
unknown, is all bays, towers, turrets and pointed
windows but somehow doesn't quite make it to
Transylvania. Its grounds are spectacular, and date
from the earlier, Georgian, house on the site, when
the steep slope of the Denburn was first terraced and
planted.

The north side of the roadway has a group of rather
narrow fronted houses designed by the young William
04 Kelly in 1895, partly speculative. 62 **Rubislaw Den
North** was Kelly's own house. No. 68 by George
Coutts, c. 1910 has horizontal bands of windows, a
broad bay balancing the gable and a recessed doorway
within a pointed arched opening, ornamented by a
pair of small heraldic shields.

205 46 Rubislaw Den North
R. Leslie Rollo and D. P. Hall, 1936
Taking the Arts and Crafts ideals as its guide,
especially Voysey in the north-corridor plan, the three
main rooms per floor are arranged on the sunny street
side, with service in the north-west corner. A large
lounge-hall with an ample staircase runs along the
back of the house.

Houses in the South Den are more visible, as they
have their major gardens in front.

Top: 4 Rubislaw Den North.
Above: Rubislaw Den House.
Below and left: 46 Rubislaw Den
North.

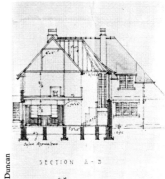

Above: 2 Rubislaw Den South.
Below: Old Rubislaw House.

206 2 Rubislaw Den South

Arthur Clyne, 1899

Fairly conventional to Forest Road (although with a decapitated gable), the entrance side is emphasised by the chimneys and staircase window, in pink granite and smooth white granite. Its mirror image stands opposite, making a handsome gateway for this side of the Den. Opposite, in **Forest Road**, are a pair of houses by the same architect whose curved *Dutch* gables with big semi-circular windows terminate the vista from Rubislaw Den South.

Note the towered and castellated **no. 32**, by Brown and Watt, the delightfully wooded **62**, R. G. Wilson, 1901 and especially **no. 72**, an early example of conservation. This highly ornamented and unusually small house originally stood, with its pair, at the entrance to the Duthie Park in Ferryhill, but was moved here when the main approach to the city was widened in 1937.

208 Queen's Road

Many notable houses. James Matthews' **11 Queen's Road**, 1875; the group **8-12 Queen's Road** by Duncan McMillan 1876; **23 Queen's Road**, now part of Albyn School, designed in 1879 by Matthews and Mackenzie.

209 50 Queen's Road

J. B. Pirie, 1886

Pirie's masterpiece. The first floor bay is supported by a large *splayed* (and decorative) pier, augmented in the gable by a pointed arch with glazing, and gothic tracery. The gable is joined to a bold asymmetrical front chimney, carried through to the other side, and thence to the tablet over the door axis. A fat ornamental corner turret has Pirie's absurd overscaled caps. The stair tower visible on the east side behind a

I wished to preserve Old Rubislaw House when I feued the ground on which it stood. I found I could have made a nice residence of the old building, by preserving the original walls, and leaving the exterior almost unchanged; but this was not to be, as it stood in the way of straightening Queen's Road, was not in line with the other houses, and my feu-Charter put a period to its existence and decreed that it must go. The only relics of the old house worth preserving in the new, were the steps leading up to the front door, which are now placed at the Conservatory door, and the Entrance Door lintel moulded and inscribed as under: A. 1675 F.

This has been placed over the arch of the kitchen door, and will there survive the life of the new House of Rubislaw. I should have liked to preserve the Skene coat of arms over the front door, but this was removed before I came into possession, and I am sorry I have not been able to recover it, perhaps I may yet, who knows?
John Morgan, *Memoirs.*

Brogden

Jenkins and Marr
Still in practice after more than a century the firm was founded by George Gordon Jenkins (1848-1923) known for his farm buildings and bridges, and George Marr, the surviving partner of G. & G. Marr whose farm practice was based at Udny, Aberdeenshire. They joined forces in 1878. The firm has consistently employed very talented juniors, and their reputation was established by the largely self-taught Harbourne MacLennan (1871-1951) whose talent is shown in the Masonic Temple, Crown Street of 1910. Other notable work by the firm is the Grill, 213 Union Street; 100 Queen's Road of 1927; and Chevron Oil Company, Altens of 1980.

Left: 50 Queen's Road.
Below: 90 Queen's Road.
Bottom: 177B Queen's Road.

Brogden

John & Marion Donald

stepped and sloped screen wall, is finished at the second floor level as a band of windows, below the *turret* roof with its finial. Even in the rear of the building, which can be glimpsed from Spademill Lane, with its large hipped dormer, and band of windows which lights Morgan's famous library, betrays the hand of a skilled designer.

210 **Nos. 90, 92** and **94 Queen's Road**, 1900, were designed by George Coutts. Beyond Anderson Drive, past Allan Ross and Allan's Kepplestone premises for Robert Gordon's Institute, 1959, and Jenkins and Marr's **100 Queen's Road**, 1927 is the great hole that was Rubislaw Quarry, which provided the granite for most of the buildings in Aberdeen. Opposite the
211 Quarry, **177 Queen's Road** was designed by A. G. R. Mackenzie for his daughter — a rather Georgian house. Tucked into the garden is John and Marion Donald's own charming and roomy house of 1983.

179 Queen's Road, Kepplestone House,
A. Marshall Mackenzie, is a regular 18th century two-storey house to which Mackenzie added a wing and bays.

St Luke's.

222 Queen's Road.

212 **St Luke's**
Viewfield Road (now the Gordon Highlanders Regimental museum)
Originally Kepplestone Cottage, c. 1800 extended by Dr William Kelly for the painter Sir George Reid, it is a romantic L-plan composition — two storeys, whitewashed with black painted woodwork, large studio windows rising up into the roof, and a stair tower with a shallow peaked roof.

213 **222 Queen's Road**
R. G. Wilson, 1909
A forward looking Arts and Crafts house with shaped granite gables punching through an overhanging roof, asymmetrical chimney, bands of windows at ground level and an overscaled Mannerist doorway.

214 **Angusfield House**
226 Queen's Road, R. G. Wilson, 1904
Pedimented pavilions with recessed centre section, crisp white granite quoins and cills contrasting with rougher ashlar, a very handsome doorway with broken pediment, and garlands on the round window above.

215 **Hazlehead Flats**
City Architects Department, 1963-64
Built in the teeth of local opposition this local authority scheme is architecturally the most pleasing of Aberdeen's flirtation with high rise building. Although the details and composition are strong the scheme's great advantage lies in the site planning which skilfully exploited existing shelter belts and farmland of Hazlehead House park.

Brogden

Angusfield House.

Brogden

Bungalows

From about 1910, and then in a rush after 1920, the **bungalow** became the favourite house type, and in many places achieved distinction. This can be seen in many sections of Aberdeen besides Queen's Road, for example **204 Springfield Road** (E. L. Williamson), a **moderne** version. The section of Anderson Drive to either side of Queen's Road is characteristic. On the east side of **Anderson Drive** are a group of individually designed bungalows: **nos. 10** and **12** are similar. Canted bays (with pediments) flank a horseshoe arched doorway (or square headed) with two piended dormers (or one central dormer) above. Tall slender chimneys mark the ends of the houses.

The Chalet

4 Anderson Drive, G. Fordyce, 1902
The earliest and most splendid bungalow: much larger than the others. Its shallow pitched roof rises from all sides past dormer windows, and is finished by a skylight in the centre. A half-timbered gable to the south (pebble-finished and plastered), a shallow canted bay and a corner window (to allow residents to glimpse visitors) are capped by chimneys rising seemingly from all sides. **51 Anderson Drive** onwards, by T. Scott Sutherland, 1936, are smaller and more typical of the type.

The Chalet.

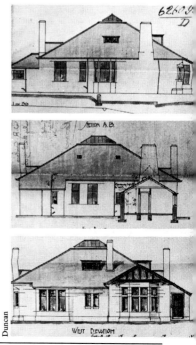

Duncan

Brig o' Balgownie, and Cottoun of
Balgownie, and the North Sea.

Aberdeen is uniquely fortunate in having two
beautiful rivers within the city when either would
have put it amongst the blessed. The Don and the
Dee have different characters although they are
roughly the same size. Because of a steeper fall in
level as the Don approaches the sea, it became the
natural site for water powered mills. Such industrial
character as Aberdeen has is best seen on its banks.
Paper and woollen mills with other industries, dot
thickly wooded steep slopes, with older settlements
such as the Cottoun of Balgownie, still a recognisable
hamlet. 20th century housing estates occupy the south
side, whereas farms and estates lie to the north. The
eastern end is fast expanding as the Bridge of Don
section of the city. Further west, and north, the old
villages of Bucksburn and Dyce are still discernable
despite the more or less continuous ribbon
development.

With the Bridge's great age,
romantic stories abound — such as
the awful proverb
Brig o' Balgownie, wight's thy wa',
Wi a wife's ae son,
An' a mare's ae foal,
Doon shalt thou fa!
which Byron remembered and
which made him *pause to cross it
and yet lean over it with a childish
delight, being an only son, at least by
my mother's side.* It is fortunate for
poetry, and the subsequent safety
of the bridge, that he had forgotten
the part about being mounted on
the only foal of a mare.

220 **Brig o' Balgownie**
Richard Cementarius, 1314-18
Until 1827, the ancient Brig, narrow and steeply
pitched above its single pointed arch, was the only
route into Aberdeen from the north. Built by Richard
Cementarius, the first Provost of Aberdeen (and also
since the arch is said to be identical in profile to the
upper vault of Drum Castle, credited with building
the keep at Drum), it was largely rebuilt at the
beginning of the 17th century, repaired in the 19th

century, and the approaches widened and buttressed in 1912. Its situation is very picturesque.

At either end of the Bridge are the old houses of **Cottoun of Balgownie**, sympathetically conserved and restored. The oldest, on the north-west side of Don Street, is the **Chapter House** of 1653. There are two cottages of 1772 (1 and 2 Rocky Bank) plus other late 18th and 19th century additions. The group is continued north of Brig o' Balgownie as one and two-storey cottages, mostly early 19th century.

Aberden City Library

By a series of somewhat shady deals, Sir Alexander Hay acquired some of the grants which before the Reformation had paid for religious observances, and in return for these he promised to set aside a sum for the repair of the Brig o' Balgownie, which is duly recorded on a plaque on the bridge.

Anno 1603 Dominus Alex Hay Clericus Registri ex innaio in rempublicam amore £26-8-6 Scoticos ex quibusdam angelis quotannis ad Aberdoniam huic fabricae sustendandae dedicavi.

Thus was the Bridge of Don Fund founded, from the princely sum of £2.28 sterling. The annual payment, prudently managed and invested by the Depute Town Clerk of Aberdeen, provided enough in the Fund to build a new Bridge downstream.

Brogden

Brogden

Top: Brig o' Balgownie from the east.
Middle: Chapter House.
Left: Cottoun of Balgownie.

Bridge of Don
John Smith, 1827
Designed with Thomas Telford as consultant and
John Gibb as executant engineer, the flat roadway of
the new bridge proved a considerable improvement on
the steep Brig o' Balgownie. It is carried on five
segmental semi-circular arches, marked at parapet level
by the projecting refuges. When the Bridge was
widened to accommodate heavier traffic in 1958
Smith's masonry was duplicated.

221   **The Seaton Flats**, 1965-70, by the City Architect's
Department are identical square towers in a grassy
setting at the top of the King's Links.

Bridge of Don has grown considerably in the last
few years, and the many houses built for sale have
attracted relatively young families. The streets
immediately north of the river were built in the 1930's
the home ground of Stewart, locally famous builder of
bungalows between the World Wars. Their
222 headquarters at **38 Ellon Road** (as King Street north of
the Don is known) is a two-storey granite building
whose segmental pediment, and simplified
composition makes it specially attractive to late 20th
century eyes. Bridge of Don has all the qualities to be
expected of a new and largely residential suburb.

Barracks of the Gordon Highlanders
Soon to be vacated, most blocks are Ministry of
Defence standard in granite. The central parade
square which faces Ellon Road is ornamented by an
enormous, splendidly coloured shield.

223 **Gray Watts & Co**
Thomson Taylor Craig and Donald, 1967
The design exploits the warehouse rooflights to give a
pleasing skyline, the office block at the end a sensible
part of the whole. There is mature planting between
the factory and the road. Much newer, and much
more spectacular although disappointing is the
224 **Aberdeen Exhibition and Conference Centre**,
Maskell and Crawford, 1985.

Top to bottom:
Bridge of Don.
38 Ellon Road.
Gordon Highlanders Regiment
    Barracks.
Gray Watt's & Co.

To the north on the Parkway, **Baker Oil Tool (UK) Ltd** offices and warehouse by Thomson Taylor Craig and Donald, 1977, has recently received a handsome extension by Robert Hurd and Partners. Further on, on Denmore Road, but visible from the Ellon Road Lister Drew's **Donside House** for ODCC shows how attention to detail and composition lifts a shed warehouse out of the ordinary.

At the edge of the city, fast being overtaken by brightly coloured warehouses with improbable names, 225 is the old **Mill of Mundurno**; typical of those that have been lost. L-shaped in plan, it is roughly one-and-a-half-storeys high, with walls of whitewash rubble and a slate roof. The mill wheel and other machinery are still in place, as is the wooden lade which carries the water to the wheel.

Donside House.

Below: Baker Oil Tool.
Bottom: Mill of Mundurno.

125

Tillydrone.

Benholm's Lodging was only moved to Tillydrone in 1964, previously standing in the heart of the city where Putachieside and the Netherkirkgate branched downward to the Green, and to St Nicholas respectively. For much of its life, it had been known as the Wallace Tower; perhaps because it, like its namesake at Edinburgh Castle was a corruption of Well House, or more probably, because the praying knight which can be seen in the recess above the armorial panel, was taken to be Sir William Wallace by those Aberdonians who passed daily by. Unfortunately, the figure was only placed on Benholm's Lodging in the middle of the 18th century, by John Niven, a tobacco dealer and snuff maker; and may indeed have originated in St Nicholas' Kirk.

Right: Benholm's Lodging.

226 **Benholm's Lodging**, 1610
A very small *Z* plan tower house, three-storeys high with round towers on the east and west sides. Except for the solecism of being unharled, it is the very picture of a miniature North-East castle, and is a valuable addition to Tillydrone.

227 **Tillydrone Housing Estate**
City Architects Department, 1968-75
A mixed development of high blocks of flats and terraces — harled walls, low pitched tile roofs, heavy timber eaves and large windows.

Powis House
11 Powis Circle, George Jaffray, 1802
Two-storeys harled with granite dressings, its centre bay enriched by pediment and pilasters, there is a Venetian window above a classical porch. It is now at the heart of the Powis Community Centre.

Powis Estate

In the 1930s, the grounds of Powis House became a local authority housing estate, both to house an increasing population, and partly to rehouse Aberdonians from slum clearance in Gallowgate and Broad Street. Powis and the other and earlier Donside Schemes — **Woodside, Tanfield** and **Middlefield** — were all the product of the City Architect's Department, and all possess similar architectural features. They formed the second phase of the mammoth rehousing programme which had begun in the 1880s, and had already produced the characteristic Aberdeen tenement: this time on officially approved *garden city* lines of not more than 12 houses per acre (although densities increased in the '30s). Streets were to be wide and curving, there were to be gardens, playgrounds and other open space; and there was a positive emphasis on good plumbing.

The Donside Schemes are largely made up of tenements of three or four rooms, arranged in three storeys, with a staircase common to six tenement flats. The architects modelled the blocks using bay windows, grouped gables, and by stepping back and forward with an artistic self-consciousness in contrast to the earlier tenements which rose cliff-like from the pavement. **Powis** is granite with plain *Georgian* windows and occasional bay windows emphasised stair doors by framed panels set above them in the old Scottish manner.

Woodside, alas not a happy place now, is both harled and granite. There are more Moderne flourishes here: parapets raised in steps towards the centre of blocks of tenements, and emphasised at the centres by vertical strip windows. At the corners, the staircase window acts as the junction between two blocks, and use paired chimney stacks in the composition. This detail can be found in the ashlar **Tanfield** and more noticeably in the harled **Hayton**, and **Middlefield** Schemes.

Cattofield, despite hot local opposition, was built in the 1920s based on Kelly's designs for Torry. His post as Director of Housing was also taken by A. B. Gardner when he succeeded as City Architect in 1923.

On Anderson Drive, a number of small blocks of four flats each, designed so as to resemble semi-detached houses were built. Sometimes they are joined to form short terraces, and occasionally they go so far as a flat roof.

Top to bottom:
Woodside.
Tanfield.
Cattofield.
Anderson Drive.

229 **Grandholm Mill,** from 1792

Attempts to exploit the Don industrially began in 1696, with paper making at Gordon Mills, just upstream of Brig o' Balgownie. Successful paper making began at Stoneywood in 1771, and in the early

RCAHMS

Brogden

19th century more factories were established opposite Woodside. Little survives from this period, although a waterwheel of 1819 is now at the Royal Scottish Museum in Edinburgh. Grandholm Mill, whose tall warehouse block dates from 1792, still survives as the famous Crombie Woollen Mill.

Woodside

The prosperity of lower Donside was greatly helped by the construction of the Aberdeenshire Canal (1795-1807), which began at Waterloo Quay, to swing around the east and north edges of Aberdeen, along the Don as far as Inverurie. Where the canal approached the Don there grew up in the early 19th century a long straggling settlement known as **Woodside**. In due course the canal was replaced by the railway, confirming Woodside's linear nature. Lately much of its early character has disappeared with the widening of the road.

A few, generally two-storey, buildings survive along Great Northern Road. At the east end of Tanfield Walk is a surviving fragment of early 19th century cottages, and the 1830 **Roman Catholic Chapel** in style of Archibald Simpson — a low rectangular block with segmental arched windows and broad 230 overhanging eaves. **Woodside Community Centre**, City Architects.Department, 1983, is a long wedge — in probably equal parts due to a stringent budget, the fear of damage by vandals, and a predilection for elemental design. The late 1920's **Trustee Savings**

Top: Woodside Mill in the early 19th century.
Above: Grandholm Mill.

128

Bank, by Dr William Kelly, is typically sharp
231 grandeur in miniature. The original **Parish Church**
designed 1829 by Archibald Simpson is a large
rectangle with pediment to Queen Street, and a large
arched entry. Before it could be paid for the
Disruption took away the Minister and most of the
congregation. Litigation about who should honour the
debt followed: the church building was auctioned and
thus became the Free Church. It has been recently
converted to a block of flats.

New Parish Church
Archibald Simpson, 1846-49
This building is more romantic, its broad overhanging
eaves and north clock tower importing an Italianate
character. Arthur Clyne's charming **Anderson Library**
of 1883 is nearby in Clifton Road.

On the north side of Great Northern Road local
authority housing in tall and short blocks is set
amongst the wooded slopes to the Don. On the south,
232 a series of widely spaced similar blocks of flats, by the
City Architect's Department display '50s detail —
splayed entrances, frequent changes of material and
good planting.

Top: Woodside Parish Church,
Simpson's original design.
Above: Anderson Library.
Left: New Parish Church.

Above: Twin Spires Creamery.
Right: The Castle.

St Machar's Episcopal Church.

233 Woodside House

Mugiemoss Road, c. 1850

Small, plain classical laird's house with a ruined stable block of 1797, with pepper pot turrets, and a raised and battlemented central section. Known as **The Castle**, latterly it served as a dormitory for the apprentices at Woodside Works.

234 Twin Spires Creamery

J. A. O. Allan Ross and Allan, 1959

An almost high-tech factory, rather poorly maintained, its main feature a tall glazed central section exposing the workings of the building, *balanced* by a steel chimney with spiral anti-eddy flue.

Aberden City Library

235 Bucksburn Church

Possibly by William Henderson, 1843-44

Built as a Free Church, with the pulpit, unusually, at the front of the church, its tall pointed windows have diamond shaped panes picked out in white painted lead, lending a delicacy to an otherwise severely rectangular block.

236 St Machar's Episcopal Church

Old Meldrum Road, A. Marshall Mackenzie, 1878

Simple, and rather jewel-box like, especially with its large circular west window. Interesting mural paintings by Douglas Strachan, 1904. **Old Schools**, Stoneywood Road, are thought to be by James Matthews: a symmetrical Gothic composition whose gabled and bellcotted centre is flanked by a pair of two-storey school houses, harled with stone margins.

Stoneywood House

James Matthews, 1849

Built for the paper manufacturer Alexander Pirie, Matthews (or his client), chose the Jacobean style for its historical and poetic powers.

237 **Newhills Church**
John Smith, 1829
A severity lightened only by the simple wooden
tracery of its windows. Smith also designed the
contemporary Manse and Manse Cottage. The session
house is 1866 by William Henderson. The stabilised
ruin of Old Newhills Church dates from 1663.

238 **Dyce**
Dyce, the last of the Donside villages, has quite
outgrown itself, to become one of the most modern
parts of the city. **Old Dyce Church**, (2 miles north-
west of Dyce high above a crook in the Don) from the
13th century, is a long, simple building in which
fragments of its earlier form can be detected, such as
the remains of a moulded Gothic doorcase in the
south wall, and a number of symbol stones in the east
wall. The Watch House is a curious survival from the
early 19th century, providing shelter for those who
kept watch over the newly interred to foil the *body
snatchers* who sold bodies to anatomists. One such
anatomy room which functioned in St Andrew Street,
was attacked by an angry mob in the 1830s.

Dyce has become a residential suburb, with a
number of modern factories to the south-east and
west. Dyce Aerodome dates from the 1920s, nothing
of that period surviving. Until quite recently, there
was little physical manifestation of the airport. Apart
from the odd shed, Dyce was best known for the
national weather reports. Within the last ten years all
that has changed. Air traffic, especially helicopters,
has increased dramatically and a new terminal was
built on the west side, thus effectively detaching the
airport from Dyce.

Below: Dyce Airport Terminal.
Bottom: Air Écosse.

239 **Dyce Airport**
Robert Matthew Johnson-Marshall and Partners, 1978
Long, horizontal and relatively low, its cladding of
beige metal panels retains its smartness despite the
fact that — like most airport buildings — it is
constantly being extended. The cake-like control tower
is by Sir Frederick Snow and Partners.

Some of the oil related shed buildings in the nearby
Kirkhill Industrial Estate have a quite surprising
elegance and power, notably **Thalossa Offshore
Scotland Ltd,** Dyce Drive, by Michael Gilmour
Associates 1983; Oliver Humphries' **Whirly Bird
Service Centre**, Howe Moss Drive of 1984; or the
Expro North Sea Ltd headquarters, Kirkhill Place
by G. R. M. Kennedy & Partners, also of 1984. But
undoubtedly the best of the group is Michael
240 Gilmour's **Air Écosse** Offices of 1978 on the east side
of the Airport at Fairburn Terrace, Dyce.

Brogden

Michael Gilmour

Wellington Bridge and Aberdeen in
1850.

The Dee has two very distinct characters: below
Craiginches it is either industrial (fish processing or
light services on the north shore) or has been diverted
and developed to make the Harbour: to the west,
Deeside is residential.

241 Wellington Suspension Bridge

Captain Samuel Brown and John Smith, 1829
The second of the Dee bridges, it connects Ferryhill
with the high bank of Craiglug to the south, and was
meant to link the expanding Aberdeen to
Kincardineshire more directly than the long trek up to
the Bridge of Dee by the Hardgate. John Smith was
responsible for the pylons and approaches and it was
supervised by James Abernethy.

The elegant new **Queen Elizabeth Bridge**, 1983,
by Grampian Regional Council Roads Department,
with its three rather tense segmental arches and tilt
from south to north, conveys more dynamism than the
older bridge.

Queen Elizabeth Bridge.

242 **Duthie Park** (W. R. McElvie, 1881), is a suitable beginning to residential Deeside. Originally the site of Arthurseat, an early 19th century villa, and the first of the Deeside pocket lairdships, it was left by Miss Charlotte Duthie to the city to form a park, opened by the Princess Beatrice in 1883. Besides the **Winter Gardens** (City Architects Department, 1972), various pieces of architecture are to be found in the Park. A **Cistern House** of 1706 was moved here from Fountainhall in 1903, and three years later the tall Peterhead granite **Obelisk**, designed by James Giles and Alexander Ellis in 1860 to honour the memory of Sir James McGrigor was transferred here from Marischal College. Near Riverside Drive is a fragment of the *old* **Cast Iron Footbridge** which crossed the Denburn near the Triple Kirks, before Rosemount Viaduct was built in 1886.

243 **Kincorth** from 1937

Sir Frank Mears' **George VI Bridge** of 1939, faced in rusticated granite blocks, leads to Kincorth, offered for feuing as early as the 1890s. The result of a 1937 national competition promoted by Tom Scott Sutherland and won by R. Gardner Medwin and others, it was laid out pre-war, and built post World War II as a local authority housing estate. Laid out on Garden City principles, curving streets follow the line of the hill overlooking the Dee. There is a school, and group of shops at the centre. The buildings are two-storey granite and slate, *traditional* in design. Municipal gardening can be seen to good advantage here, and there are some nice touches such as the continuation of the line of the Bridge of Dee up the hill as a series of garden ramps.

244 **Bridge of Dee**, 16th century

Projected as early as the 14th century, the bridge was begun by the great Bishop William Elphinstone, but at his death in 1514, although material, including dressed stone from Morayshire, was at hand, construction had hardly begun. Building in earnest began in 1518 under Gavin Dunbar's bishopric and was carried out by Alexander Galloway and Thomas Franche. Its flat roadway, originally about 4 metres wide, is carried on seven ribbed arches, marked by refuges and cutwaters and decorated with coats of arms and inscriptions. At either end are tall conical ornaments with ball finials.

The chapel near the north end, and a port on the Kincardineshire side were both removed in the late 18th century. Restored in 1720, in 1840 it was widened by John Smith, the City Architect, who had recommended replacing the Bridge with a new one. The Town Council demurred so Smith removed the

Curtis Green's drawing of the Bridge of Dee.

133

Bridge of Dee.

facings on the west side, widened the Bridge on that side, and then replaced them.

Nearby, in Riverside Drive, is the old **Ruthrieston Pack Bridge** of 1693. It was moved 30 metres eastwards in 1923.

The northern banks of the Dee had attracted Aberdonians as early as the 1840s when **Cults** and **Pitfodels** were the sites of villas. With the coming of the Deeside Railway in 1853, and the improvement of the old Braemar Road a necklace pattern of development was established — a series of settlements, based on old hamlets or villages, served by stations, a few shops and churches but distinct and separate from each other, all enjoying views of the Dee and Kincardineshire.

Ferryhill was the first of these Deeside suburbs.
245 The next stop on the old railway was **Ruthrieston** (sometime *Ruddreistoun*) now swallowed up by the city. Ruthrieston is an old hamlet, and probably grew up in association with the building of the Bridge of Dee. It had an annual fair, the showy Pack Bridge, **Outseats House** (395 Hardgate) c. 1800 and groups of cottages along the road to Aberdeen. Some, such as the **Abergeldie Inn, Ruthrieston Lodge** (540 Holborn Street), and a small group at the Bridge of Dee survive. **Lorne Buildings**, 1870, were built for the employees of the new waterworks then being brought in from Banchory.

In 1875, James Forbes Beattie proposed a scheme for building a broad carriage drive next to the river, to be ornamented by large villas, with simpler houses on Holburn Street, facing towards the river. This succeeded in part. There are several houses from this period — The **Park Hotel**, designed in 1885 by Matthews and Mackenzie for William Hall, the great ship builder. The building of **Ruthrieston School** by Jenkins and Marr, 1880s, changed the character of Beattie's layout. An art deco wing (although built in the '50s) by J. A. O. Allan Ogg and Allan and 20th century bungalows complete the scene.

Park Hotel.

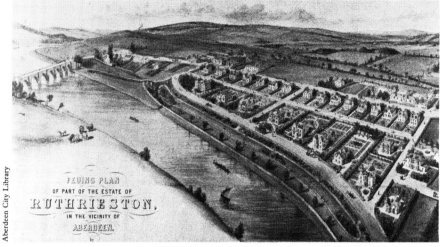

Above: Forbes Beattie's proposed layout for Ruthrieston.
Left: Broomhill Church.

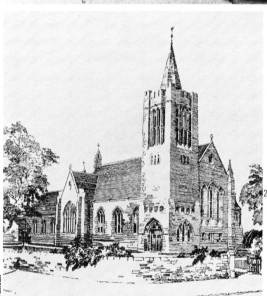

In 19th century Aberdeen, churches usually came in pairs. In 1876, the Kirk established its presence in Ruthrieston, first in the Old School, then in an *Iron Kirkie*, and from 1890 in A. Marshall Mackenzie's building on Holburn Street.

Mannofield

By 1860 the old turnpike road to Braemar had been diverted from its original course, Broomhill Road, northwards to Mannofield from where it joined the Great Western Road. **Mannofield** then began its development as a suburb served by both the Deeside railway, and shortly by the tramway.

246 **Ruthrieston** must have been a rather unruly place, and typical of unruly places, it attracted a powerful preacher, Mungo Parker, then convalescing in the district. He began his mission (being of Free Church persuasion) in a pub by the Fords of Dee, and then moved on to a converted cottage. His preaching brought congregations from Aberdeen. His memory was nurtured by the local congregation after his death, so that by 1872 they had appointed a new minister and secured designs from James Matthews for a Church on Broomhill Road. This relatively simple building was extended in 1900 by Alexander Brown and George Watt, and their corner tower is worth special attention. Its very short spire with the four pinnacles gives the building a curious profile.

In the 18th century Robert Balmanno, a Quaker, acquired a piece of ground which had hitherto been called *The Foul Moors* on account of the barren nature of the soil. This ground was enclosed by Balmanno and brought under intensive cultivation for the growing of fruit. As a result of this activity, a small community grew up on the Countesswells Road at the South West of Balmanno's *enclosure*, or as it was called *Balmanno's field* — later contracted to Mannofield.

Fenton Wyness, *City by the Grey North Sea.*

Right: Friendville.
Below: Thorngrove.
Bottom: Mannofield Church.

247 Friendville, 1773

The *beau ideal* of a small Georgian manor house. Two-storeys, five bay, with a central gable, it was heavily restored with a pantiled roof in 1943 by Fenton Wyness for William Bell. Specially notable is the Tempietto with wrought iron dome which stands opposite the front door.

248 Thorngrove

(500 Great Western Road), J. Russell Mackenzie, 1867 Mackenzie's own house, its steep gabled dormered roof conceals a full bedroom floor. The Gothic details of the dormers, and the steepness of the roof pitches gives it a *storybook* air. It was the first house in Aberdeen to have electric light in 1894.

249 Mannofield Church

Jenkins and Marr, 1882

An attenuated tower and spire based like most Aberdeen churches, on St Nicholas; but nowhere else is it apparently so tall and so slender. Since Mannofield stands at a crook in the road, its pencil thin tower is clearly visible along Great Western Road. There is a sympathetic but far from slavish addition to the south of the church by Baxter Clark and Paul.

Westwards, beyond the Aberdeenshire County Cricket Club, the only visible parts of Provost Sir Alexander Anderson's reservoir of 1864 are the short battlemented towers in its centre. There is a **New Water Filtration Plant** to the west, 1985, by Grampian Regional Council Architects Department.

250 St Francis Roman Catholic Church

Oliver Humphries, 1983

An undistinguished small church to the north was turned into a church hall, and lower down the sloping site a new sanctuary was built, on plan two squares at 45 degrees to each other. The roof rises to a point at the centre, and details from a variety of sources are pleasingly mixed.

Pitfodels, from 1859

The Pitfodels estate — lying between Aberdeen and Cults and between the Deeside Road and the River was parcelled out for sale in 1859 by James Forbes Beattie. The plots along the road were as small as one third acre (generally plots were 3 acres, and along the River were often 8 to 10 acres), and at the Aberdeen end near the Bridge of Dee, Beattie proposed villas in relatively small plots as he did later at nearby Ruthrieston. Kaimhill was to be laid out more formally.

Apart from the building of Garthdee Road, this end was not built up until after World War II, when it became a satellite suburb on the pattern of Kincorth. A distant echo to Forbes Beattie's proposal is an interesting pre-War civic group associated with the 251 former **Aberdeen Crematorium** (City Architects Department, 1937). The Crematorium, block-like in rock-faced granite stands in its garden while opposite it, and on axis, is a group of white harled semi-detached houses with red tile roofs, large dormer windows and curved bay windows. They are grouped formally about a *village green* and are connected by white screen walls.

Kaimhill Gardens.

A group of pre-War wooden houses by the City architect look as fresh as if they had been constructed within the last five years. Clad in cedar shingles they have crisp white woodwork and red tile roofs. John Morgan the builder tried to introduce wooden construction from Canada at the turn of the 19th and 20th centuries, but he encountered a prejudice against it.

But Beattie's scheme for the rest of Menzies estate was carried out. It became, especially the plots by the river, the ideal suburb for those few who could afford such style — the Aberdeen merchant princes; and as 19th century wealth liked to express itself in architecture, a number of interesting buildings resulted.

252 **Norwood**, 1859

Norwood.

Norwood may incorporate earlier work, as it is on the site of Menzies of Pitfodels' own house; the ancient motte of Pitfodels Castle survives east of the house. Low pedimented gables flank the front entrance porch, the architectural features picked out in sandstone, the rest harled standing on a granite base. Although symmetrical at the entrance, the effect of Norwood now is asymmetrical, even rambling, due to

K

J. Russell Mackenzie's reworking of the house in 1881. The interiors by W. Scott Morton are quite superb: a long hall (a sort of lounge-hall before its time) runs through the house and occupies the original right hand bay. From this a very grand staircase opens to the left and is lit by a coved lantern in the roof. The woodwork is of the best, its richness enhanced by extraordinary anaglypta paper masquerading, and very effectively, as Spanish stamped leather. This continues into a drawing room added by Mackenzie. Norwood was converted into a hotel in 1972 by M. F. Beattie and W. Cowie. A Loudonesque Gate Lodge, 1859, survives as does the woodland garden, probably laid out by Forbes Beattie.

Drumgarth.

Brogden

253 **Drumgarth**
Architect unknown, 1859
Single-storey, gables to either side of the entrance, and an upper floor concealed within the broad eaved roof. In the grounds is the Windmill, resited from Windmill Brae opposite the old entrance to Aberdeen at the Green, and brought here in 1859. It is circular, with a conical roof surmounted by a weathervane of 1760. There is a 1680 lintel stone.

Garthdee latterly became the home of architect Tom Scott Sutherland, one of the last of the merchant princes. Despite severe disablement he became a prolific house, bungalow and cinema architect and was also, at one time, a director of forty different companies, including being a founder director of Caledonian Associated Cinemas. He became a thrusting Housing Convener in the late '30s, responsible for changing city policy toward flats, for Rosemount Square and for the Kincorth competition. He gave the estate of Garthdee with endowment to the Aberdeen School of Architecture which now bears his name. In 1956, his firm added the glass-walled studios facing south, on the east wing. In 1969 this wing became part of a new quadrangle of studios and lecture theatres by Thomson Taylor Craig and Donald.

254 **Inchgarth**
A. Marshall Mackenzie, 1897
Two-storey, granite with a classical porch, it incorporates work from 1859. Inchgarth Cottage, in the grounds also dates from 1859.

255 **Garthdee House**
William Smith, 1872
High above the Dee in about 20 acres of well-wooded grounds, it is a granite, asymmetrical Jacobean composition derived ultimately from William Burn's design for Auchmacoy House. The heart of Garthdee House is the two-storeyed, skylit hall, a grand staircase (with stained glass window) leading to an upper arcaded, richly ornamented gallery.

Albert Duguid

Right: Garthdee House.

256 Grays School of Art
Michael Shewan (as successor to T. Scott Sutherland),
1966
Set on a bluff west of Garthdee House, the School
does homage to the architecture of Mies van der Rohe
in Chicago. It is a symmetrical composition in black
painted steel and glass, raised slightly from the ground
and originally entered up a flight of floating steps in
the centre. It is articulated by external steel beams
used as columns. To the south are two lower wings
whose roofs are supported by great girders, and as
Mies had done at Crown Hall at IIT in Chicago a few
years earlier, here expressed as part of the
architecture. Between wings is an elevated open
courtyard whose south side is *closed* by the woods and
fields of Kincardineshire. Gray's is probably the best
mid 20th century building in Aberdeen.

Above: Gray's School of Art.
Below: Woodbank.
Bottom: Wellwood.

On the north side of the Deeside Road, several villas
existed before the coming of the railway. The most
257 prominent of these is **Woodbank**, and although this
dates from 1848, it is the work of 1875-78 which gives
it its character — a picturesque composition above a
sweeping terrace of towers and elaborately
bargeboarded gables. To the west is a large but fairly
unobstrusive games hall, added when Woodbank
became the Shell Training Centre.

Brogden

258 Wellwood, c. 1840
A cottage with a Tudor arch for its doorway, bay
windows to either side with gables above. Later, a
west wing with central gable with decorated
bargeboards and Jacobean porch was added.

259 Morkeu House (now Greenridge)
Archibald Simpson, 1845
In a cottage style like most of the houses in this
district, its later porte cochere by George Watt, 1910,
loggia and terrace belie its original simplicity.

Brogden

Top: Morrison's Bridge.
Above: Loirsbank.
Right: Cults House.

260 Morrison's Bridge
John Smith, 1836
The Rev. George Morrison, minister of Banchory Devenick Kirk, on the south side of the Dee had a number of parishioners in Cults, on the north bank. For the benefit of their souls, he had John Smith build a suspension footbridge. The pylons are cast iron, plain doric columns on stone piers. The river's course has shifted southwards, undermining one of the abutments. In a comic game of official *pass the potato*, no one can be found to be responsible for the bridge's repair. At the north end of **Morrison's Bridge** is the old **Pumping Station**, part of Aberdeen Waterworks, and built by William Smith in 1864. In temple form, with centre door and flanking windows it is now a

261 house. Nearby is **Loirsbank**, a row of flat roofed houses in the '50s modern fashion by Mackie Ramsay and Taylor. The living rooms are on the first floor and garages below. Large sheets of glass are contrasted to vertical boarding.

262 Cults House, 18th- early 19th century was altered by William Henderson in about 1860. The garden wall of thick rubble with sloped coping is 18th century, as are the ball capped gatepiers.

263 Ellengowan, 1835 is a specially distinguished version of the cottage house; a main front of three bays, the central door flanked by windows, while the gable elevation has three windows with a group of three round headed windows in the attic. Pilasters and groin vault can be found in the entrance hall.

James Henderson (1809-1896) withdrew from his studies at Marischal College at his father's death in 1826. He studied architecture at the Mechanics Institute evening classes. He was briefly in partnership with his elder brother William and they shared the early work for the Free Church from 1843 almost exclusively. Besides an extensive country practice he built the charming Westfield Terrace, and the replacement of Morrison's Hall, Union Chambers 47-49 Union Street, which was designed as early as 1883 but completed in the 1890s by **William Henderson, younger**, (1829-1899) better known as architect of Union Banks all over North East Scotland.

Brogden

Left: Cults West Church.
Below: St Devenick's Episcopal Church.
Bottom: International Baptist Church, courtyard.

Brogden

87 Cults West Church
A. Marshall Mackenzie, 1915-16

A square tower, rather short with fine granite ashlar spire, leads to low nave with prominent gablets to east and west. Further along the Deeside Road is Arthur 89 Clyne's Episcopal Church, **St Devenicks** of 1902-03, cruciform in plan, its tower off centre in the south-west corner. Grey granite is mixed with pink — of which Clyne was rather fond. The interior boasts a wooden wagon roof, a wooden chancel arch, a painted glass window from St Andrews c. 1838, and a granite screen of 1849 from Perth by William Butterfield.

88   **Bieldside House** is a real curiosity. Lower half is early 19th century, plain Scots Palladian reticence: the top half was added by George Watt for himself in 1903. Iron railing, gatepiers and service buildings to the west (including the rather coarse but charming garden pavilion) are of the earlier period.

84 International Baptist Church
Earlswells Road, Cults, G. R. M. Kennedy and Partners, 1984

An interesting contemporary church which exploits the early Christian courtyard of fellowship to great advantage: axial planning holds major and minor elements together nicely.

265 Ladyhill
Bailliewells Road, A. Marshall Mackenzie, 1912
The architect's own house: single-storey with mansard
roof and dormers of varied and original design: a
slightly later lodge to match.

266 Littleways
Bailliewells Road, David Stokes, 1934
Designed for himself by the head of A. G. R.
Mackenzie's Aberdeen office, it recalls Marshall
Mackenzie's own house nearby. It restates the long,
thin, sun oriented design in almost modernist terms.
Its harled walls, pitched roof, and band of articulated
corridor windows suggests C. R. Mackintosh's
influence, although the architect himself suggests that
of W. M. Dudok.

Above: Ladyhill.
Right: Littleways.
Below: Murtle House and
Camphill Auditorium.

270 Murtle Estate
Archibald Simpson
Almost a caricature of his cottage style **Murtle
Cottage,** with absurdly tall and narrow bay windows,
it has enormous charm and is very well maintained.
271 Murtle House, also by Simpson, 1823, now the hub
of a school, is perched on a bend of the Dee. It
appears to have been designed as a round temple with
doric columns and a low dome; in fact this is a bow
within a more conventional house, but the idea that
Simpson responded to the romantic qualities of the
scene is overwhelming. This design idea was restated
in 1960 by Gabor Talló in a strong *expressionist* style
as the Camphill Auditorium, recently extended by
Camphill Architects. Within the grounds of Murtle
House and neighbouring estates which now make up
the Camphill schools are a number of other buildings
betraying the influence of Rudolf Steiner: with their
low, angular rather helmed roofs they obey their own
logic and are remarkably consistent. Nearby, **Murtle
Sawmill,** early 19th century, was one of the earliest
threshing mills in the area, converted to a restaurant.

142

Graham Benton

Left: Kippie Lodge.
Below: Culter House.

72 **Murtleden** is Edwardian in the Arts and Crafts style, with a three-storey tower, projecting bay window, and a terrace.

73 **Kippie Lodge**
A. H. L. Mackinnon, 1940
The sort of house one might easily find in America, so it is even more suitable that its recent role has been that of a clubhouse for those involved in oil. Nearby is the American School.

74 **Culter House**, from 17th century
The south-east wing, with its tower projections at the ends, and doorway with associated chimney at the centre, is the original. The other side is c. 1730 (perhaps Alexander Jaffray): a regular nine bay front of three-storeys and basement. Wings were added to north and south in 1910 by W. Dalton Ironside, and after a fire in the same year Dr William Kelly reinstated the interior using as much of the original as possible. The walled garden dates from the house's second period of about 1730, and suggests an equally important formal garden layout within. There are two pairs of gates, rusticated, with ball capped piers, and symmetrically placed gazebo and doo-cot both of square plan and pyramid roof.

Brogden

Rob Roy

Robert MacGregor (also known as Campbell) was a highland freebooter in the period after the *Glorious Revolution* of 1688 which brought in William and Mary in place of James VII. Nominally a grazier he was more likely a cattle rustler, but his education, culture and the sympathy later generations have for the beleaguered highland clan chieftains have given him the aura of a Robin Hood. In the early 18th century MacGregor was in Aberdeen visiting relations, among them the professor of medicine, to drum up support for the Jacobite cause. While walking with one of them in the Castlegate, and hearing a drum roll he became alarmed and nipped down the nearest pend. On reaching Leucher Burn at Culter he found it in spate, and as there was no bridge, he leaped across to safety. The statue commemorates this *feat*.

Right: St Peter's Church.
Below: St Peter's churchyard.

Brogden

Brogden

275 **St Peter's Church**

Peterculter, late 18th century
A typical long rectangle, with a venetian window in the west end, and round headed side windows, it has been twice altered: first by James Matthews in 1873, and later by Alexander Brown in 1895. There is a churchyard, with excellent monuments and late 18th century watch house. The manse dates from the early 18th century, but was reworked when the new Church was built. There is a two-storey addition with porch to the front, by John Lyon, 1826.

The first successful paper making was established in Peterculter in the mid 18th century by Bartholomew Smith at Culter Burn. Besides there being an hitherto untapped source of rags, there were two Colleges plus schools and a flourishing printing industry to justify the enterprise. Paper making moved to the Don in the 19th century and the Kennerty Mills were used as grain mills; at one time there was a one-man snuff mill. It produced three hundred weight per week. The 19th century mills were burned and rebuilt in the early 1940s, and they have been largely replaced recently by new houses.

276 The **Bridge of Culter Burn** by Jenkins and Marr, retains details of earlier work. North of the Bridge is a coloured, larger than life statue of Rob Roy MacGregor about to leap across the burn.

Published works consulted for this guide
The Building Chronicle; Sir Henry Alexander and others, **City of Aberdeen Housing and Town Planning**, nd; **Black Kalendar of Aberdeen**, 1878; Alexander Carlyle, **Journal of a Tour to the North of Scotland**, nd; W. D. Chapman and C. F. Riley, **Granite City**, 1952; Andrew Cluer (and R. Winram), **Aberdeen Walkin' the Mat** 1976 and 1984 editions; Daniel Defoe, **A Tour Thro' the Whole Island of Great Britain**, 1727; William Diack, **Rise and Progress of the Granite Industry of Aberdeen**, 1949; Godfrey Evans, **Polite Society in Aberdeen in the 18th Century**, nd; G. M. Fraser, **Aberdeen Mechanics Institute**, 1912; G. M. Fraser **Archibald Simpson, Architect & His Times**. A Study in the Making of Aberdeen: **Aberdeen Weekly Journal**, 5th April 1918 to 11th October 1918; G. M. Fraser, **Bridge of Dee**, 1913; Alexander Gammie, **The Churches of Aberdeen**, 1909; Cuthbert Graham, **Portrait of Aberdeen and Deeside**, 1972; Cuthbert Graham, **Historical Walk-About of Aberdeen**, nd; (Ronald Harrison) **Archibald Simpson Architect of Aberdeen 1790-1847**, 1978; Alexander Keith, **A Thousand Years of Aberdeen**, 1972; Alexander Keith, **Eminent Aberdonians**, 1984; William Kennedy, **Annals of Aberdeen**, 1818; **The Leopard**; Hugh Mackenzie, **The City of Aberdeen**, 1953; Lachlan MacKinnon, **Recollections of an Old Lawyer**, 1935; John Milne, **Topographical Antiquarian and Historical Papers in the City of Aberdeen**, 1911; James Moriarty (editor) **Aberdeen Port Handbook**, 1985; John Murray's **Handbook for Travellers in Scotland**, 1894; **Notes From the Minute Books of the Aberdeen Hammermen Incorporation**, 1892; William Robbie, **Aberdeen Its Traditions and History**, 1893; (James Robertson) **The Book of Bon Accord**, 1839; (James Rettie) **Aberdeen Fifty Years Ago**, 1868; St Machar's Cathedral **Occasional Papers**: Ronald G. Cant, **The Building of St Machar's Cathedral, Aberdeen**, 1976; Leslie J. Macfarlane, **St Machar's Cathedral in the Later Middle Ages**, 1979; and David Stevenson, **St Machar's Cathedral and the Reformation 1560-1690**, 1981; J. S. Smith, **New Light on Medieval Aberdeen**, 1985; Walter Thom, **History of Aberdeen**, 1811; George Walker, **Aberdeen Awa'**, 1897; William H. Watson, **A. Marshall Mackenzie Architect in Aberdeen**, 1985; J. M. Wilson, **Imperial Gazetteer of Scotland** nd; Fenton Wyness, **City by the Grey North Sea**, 1966; Fenton Wyness, **Aberdeen Century of Change**, 1971; and Fenton Wyness, **More Spots from the Leopard**, 1973.

Collections and Unpublished Works
Primary source material on Aberdeen's buildings is held in the City Archive in the Town House and consists of minute books, and feu charters relating to the early 19th century improvements, as well as maps, and plans. Plans and other drawings for buildings erected from c. 1870 are held in St Nicholas House. There are collections of drawings, plans and photographs at: Aberdeen Art Gallery; Aberdeen Public Library; Aberdeen University Library; and Robert Gordon's Institute of Technology, Scott Sutherland School of Architecture Library. Outside Aberdeen the best source of material is the excellent National Monument Record of Scotland in Edinburgh.

The Scottish Development Department's *Buildings of Special Architectural or Historical Interest, Aberdeen* was an indispensable aid in writing this Guide.

Apart from G. M. Fraser's excellent series of newspaper articles on Simpson (available as a collection of photocopies at the Public Library) the best body of work on Aberdeen architecture has been created in the last ten years or so by students at Scott Sutherland School of Architecture. Except for W. H. Watson's work on *A. Marshall Mackenzie* which was published in 1985 the following diploma dissertations can only be seen at the Scott Sutherland School of Architecture Library at Garthdee, or in the National Monuments Record of Scotland in Edinburgh: A. W. Cumming, **History of Aberdeen Town House**, 1975; Frank Farmer, **Early History of Union Street**, Aberdeen, 1800-1824, 1974; B. J. Finnie **History and Development of Old Aberdeen**, 1975; Charles A. Minty, **William Kelly, LLD, ARSA**, 1983, Robert E. Morris, **History and Architecture of the Damlands in Aberdeen's West End** 1802-1902, 1978; David Murray, **Robert Gordon's Hospital**, 1975; M. J. McA. Porter, **Public Buildings and Churches of John Smith in Aberdeen**, 1979; T. W. Smith, **Historical Survey of the Castlegate/Marischal Street Area of Aberdeen**, 1978; R. W. Smyth, **Archibald Simpson, His Classical Buildings in Aberdeen**, 1975; Frank Tocher, **Scottish Episcopal Churches in Aberdeen Diocese, by Sir John Ninian Cornper**, 1979.

Acknowledgements
Very many people have contributed to the writing of this Guide and it is a pleasure to acknowledge their assistance. Charles McKean and David Walker in Edinburgh and David Kinghorn, Jim Lyon and Norman Patterson in Aberdeen have read the manuscripts and provided much helpful information and encouragement. Others who have read the manuscript or large parts of it and offered much useful advice are Richard Emerson, Leslie Macfarlane, Norman Marr, David Paton, Peter Robinson, John Soutar, John Smith, Harold Watt, Bill Watson and Robin Webster.

Judith Cripps and Jamus J. K. Smith at the Town House; Albert Allen and his staff in the Planning Department; Stanley Moir, the City Architects Department at St Nicholas House; Francina Irwin at the Aberdeen Art Gallery; Judith Stones at the Archaeological Unit, Frederick Street; James Main at King's College, and the staff at the Special Collections Aberdeen University Library; Jim Duncan, Jim Fiddes, Frances Stevenson, Catherine Roberts and Linda Kennedy at RGIT libraries; the Local Section staff at Aberdeen Public Library; and Ian Gow at NMRS have all been cheerful, helpful and patient.

For individual kindness I am grateful to: Joan Allen, Messrs Alexander and Gillan, Frank Connon, Alex Duffus, Bryce Esslemont, Peter Gibb, May Miller, Graham Hunter, A. I. Macrae, Allan MacKimmie, Harry McNab, George Heddle, Diane Morgan, Messrs Paul and Williamson, Jonathan Young and A. T. McCombie.

The family of John Smith kindly provided a photograph of his portrait; and James Yule, grandson of John Morgan, has kindly allowed me to quote from the *Memoirs*.

I am very grateful indeed to Morag Beaton, Margaret Geddes and Tayona McKeown for typing and to Albert Duncan for processing photographs. Photographs and drawings were also provided by the Aberdeen Art Gallery, Aberdeen City Libraries, Aberdeen University, City of Aberdeen, the National Monuments Record of Scotland, RGIT and the Scottish Record Office, and many individuals especially Albert Duncan, David Brown, Charles McKean, and Iain Livesley to whom I am most grateful. The source of each illustration is credited alongside.

MAIN MAP

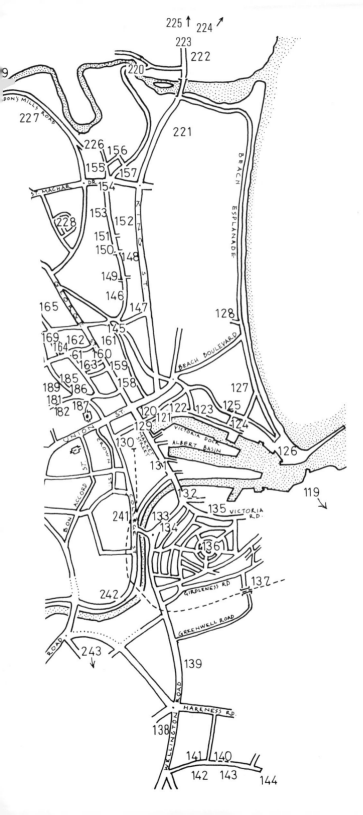

NEO CLASSICAL TOWN

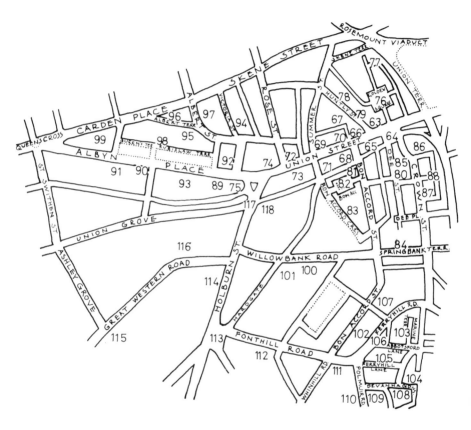

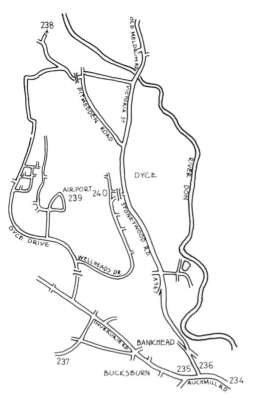

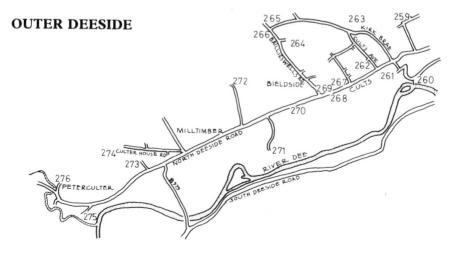

INDEX

INDEX